disinformants
the liberal battle to control information

by carlos chavarria

*This book is dedicated to my parents for their continual love
and support. Thank you, mom & dad. I love you both.*

*Special thank you for the guy who helped with chapter 7.
Thanks buddy, you know who you are.*

*To my uncle Pete, you were loved, you are missed.
Semper Fi brother.*

*Peter Allen Krebsbach
July 28, 1949 - August 25, 2020*

intro

cognitive dissonance - the state of having inconsistent thoughts, beliefs, or attitudes, especially as relating to behavioral decisions and attitude change.

doublespeak - language that deliberately obscures, disguises, distorts, or reverses the meaning of words.

gaslighting - a form of psychological manipulation in which a person or a group covertly sows seeds of doubt in a targeted individual or group, making them question their own memory, perception, or judgment, often evoking in them cognitive dissonance

thoughtcrime - an instance of unorthodox or controversial thinking, considered as a criminal offense or as socially unacceptable.

.
.
.
.
.

"Don't you see that the whole aim of Newspeak is to narrow the range of thought? In the end we shall make thoughtcrime literally impossible, because there will be no words in which to express it" - George Orwell, 1984

chapter 1: introducing the democratic party

The Democratic Party was founded by Andrew Jackson and Martin Van Buren, on January 8, 1828 after formally splitting from the previous party known as the Democratic-Republican party. The Democratic Party is the oldest political party in the U.S. and the oldest voter based political party in the world. Some of the more notable Democratic Party members have been:

Barack Obama: 44th President of the United States. First president with African-American heritage.

Hillary Clinton: Former U.S. Senator. Former Secretary of State. First female presidential candidate to win a significant number of electoral votes.

Joe Biden: 47th Vice President of the United States (under Barack Obama). 2020 democratic presidential nominee. Advocate for racial segregation in schools. Author of a 1994 crime bill, institutionalizing racism. He also thinks if you're black and don't vote for him, *"you ain't black"*.

Woodrow Wilson: 28th President of the United States. Instituted racial segregation for federal workers.

Franklin Delano Roosevelt: 32nd President of the United States. Ordered Japanese-Americans as little as 1/16th Japanese into concentration camps after seizing their homes, and their businesses. As a person of ½ Japanese ancestry I would have been forced to join them which is deeply disturbing to me. This single act destroyed thousands of lives, tore apart families, and set Japanese immigrants back generations. He also appointed a klansman to the Supreme court (see next entry).

Hugo Black: U.S. Senator. Associate Justice serving in the U.S. Supreme Court. Documented, and self-admitted Klansman.

James Buchanan: 15th President of the United States. Advocate for slave owners' rights to keep their slaves. Advocated for Kansas to allow slavery in their constitution.

Franklin Pierce: 14th President of the United States. Signed the Kansas-Nebraska Act in 1854. This repealed the Missouri Compromise and allowed new states in the Westward expansion to adopt slavery.

John Tyler: 10th President of the United States. After his presidency, advocated to let the southern states keep slavery.

In addition to those duly elected democratic political figures, there's also prominent confederate democrats such as Nathan Bedford Forrest (yes the same one referenced in the popular 90's movie Forrest Gump). Bedford joined the KKK and was elected to be the Grand Wizard of the Klan two years after its founding. An extremely high honor for a white supremacist. To be fair, late in his life, Mr. Forrest renounced his beliefs as a white supremacist. After decades spent terrorizing Americans, most of whom were freed slaves.

Then there's Wade Hampton. Hampton led a group of individuals known as the Redeemers. The Redeemers were part of a coalition of groups known as Bourbon Democrats. They used violence to gain political power and enforce white supremacy. Quite simply, they were terrorists. Their mission for 'redemption' was meant to remove Republicans and freed slaves from political power and *"enforce white supremacy"*[1] in southern states. Mr. Hampton decided to run for governor of South Carolina as a democrat. During his campaign, another Bourbon Democrat group known as

---

[1] As quoted by: https://en.wikipedia.org/wiki/Redeemers

the Red Shirts back his campaign. Who are these Red Shirts? The Red Shirts were yet another terrorist group that *"served the Democratic Party"*[2]. They sought to achieve their mission of white supremacy by disrupting elections. They actively engaged in suppressing black, and Republican votes. They used violence, and violent threats against Republicans and freed slaves to influence the election. Just like the Redeemers, the Red Shirts were the literal definition of terrorists. If this sounds familiar to anyone who experienced the 2016 and 2020 election cycles, well I'll let you be the judge. Domestic terrorism is the history of the Democratic Party. Unfortunately, the strategy of terror worked, and Hampton was elected the 77th Governor of South Carolina. He served from 1876 to 1879, and after completing his term in office as governor, he continued his political career and served two terms as a U.S. Senator representing South Carolina.

Continuing down the list, we arrive at Horatio Seymour. Seymour served as Governor of New York before and during the civil war. After the civil war, in 1868 Seymour was nominated as the democratic presidential candidate. His running mate was Frank Blair, Jr. was nominated as the democratic vice-presidential candidate. Blair is documented as being friends with Mr. Nathan Bedford Forrest, so this next fact will might make sense. The slogan for the 1868 Democratic National Convention was:

"Our Ticket, Our Motto, This Is a White Man's Country; Let White Men Rule" – Politico, July 22, 2016 via Politico.

Ladies and gentlemen, there you have it. An all-star line-up of racist democrats. There's a reason why democrats see racism in almost everything: they have to look themselves in the mirror to get ready in the morning.

---

[2] As quoted by: https://en.wikipedia.org/wiki/Wade_Hampton_III

Democrats also advocated the ending of the Freedmen's Bureau, and any government policy designed to aid blacks in the South. According to History.com:

> *"The Freedmen's Bureau, formally known as the Bureau of Refugees, Freedmen and Abandoned Lands, was established in 1865 by Congress to help millions of former black slaves and poor whites in the South in the aftermath of the Civil War."* – History.com, October 3, 2018 via A&E Television Networks

The goal of this governmental department was to provide necessities such as food, housing, and medical aid to former slaves and poor whites in Southern states after the civil war. It also attempted to establish schools for former slaves as it had been illegal for nearly all slaves, and even some free blacks to receive a formal education. This left many black Americans unable to read or write. However, these goals were never completely implemented as the Bureau was never fully funded. Lincoln was assassinated shortly after the civil war ended, and Andrew Johnson then assumed the presidency. While he honored Lincoln's memory by moving forward with the appointment of General Oliver Howard to head the bureau, he also did very little to advance the Bureau recommendations. Then about a month and a half after he was sworn in as president, Johnson made an open offer to any confederate soldier who would pledge loyalty to the union: they were to be given amnesty, full pardons, and have their property rights restored. This was probably a good olive branch to extend to the former confederate soldiers. Johnson's offer would help to reconcile the bitterness between fellow countrymen. Many of the confederate soldiers had been poor, illiterate, and were conscripted or joined the confederate army to defend their state. Remember a person's state citizenship was a much bigger part of a person's identity than it is today. Still it was a move that angered many pro-union Repbulicans.

Johnson also openly worked to undermine the newly freed slaves. Johnson became an advocate for the numerous black codes formed after the civil war ended. Black Codes were laws put into place that were specifically targeted at the newly freed slaves. They dictated what black people were and were not allowed to do. Black codes were the Jim Crow laws you've heard about. Even though the civil war had freed black people from slavery, it had not freed them from tyranny. One of the things black codes did was keep them in place as laborers on the plantations they were just freed from. Often the U.S. Army was responsible to round up former slaves and return them to the very plantations they had escaped. They would be placed on the plantations under a contract so it couldn't be called 'slavery'. Yet that's effectively what it was. For many orphaned or young 'freed' slaves these black codes were used to force them to work as apprentices under their former owners. These post-war black codes were often extensions of the very same codes and laws that existed before the civil war. They were used to govern conduct of slaves. However once slaves were free, democrats like Johnson wanted new restrictions put into place to control black people no longer shackled by slavery. It was all around disgusting and will forever stain the soul of our great nation.

The Loving v. Virginia case was centered around one of these black codes. Before the civil war, many states had implemented black codes for regulating intermarriage and miscegenation with slaves. After the war they simply changed the codes to target freed slaves. Over 20 states adopted black codes against miscegenation during the postwar years. They usually went further in restricting antebellum practices. This included eliminating the legality for a white slave owner to marry a black slave. There were also laws instituted that barred freedmen (former slaves) from receiving a donations or inheritances from a white person. These are the things democrat Andrew Johnson supported.

Some of people might be thinking, "but all that happened over a century ago. Democrats have changed."

Honestly, it's a fair point. But have they changed? Or did the Democratic Party become more nefarious? Are they simply better at hiding their true intentions? I think it's important to understand the types of people who founded the Democratic Party because it gives context to understand the modern-day democratic policies.

But let's look at a few contemporary examples of people demonstrating democrats' outstanding behaviour. And let's start with everyone's favorite Governor from Virginia, democrat Ralph Northam. For those of you who don't know, Ralph was Lieutenant Governor under Terry McAuliffe from 2014 thru 2018. He then ran for Governor and as of this writing is currently serving his first term. During his election campaign a photo was discovered of Ralph from his 1984 medical school yearbook. There are two young men in the photo, and it is unclear which of the two is Ralph. Was he the man wearing black face or was he the person in the klan robe and hood? Given the history of the Democratic Party, it really could go either way. Of course, Ralph apologized for the photo, issuing the following statement:

> *"Earlier today, a website published a photograph of me from my 1984 medical school yearbook in a costume that is clearly racist and offensive. I am deeply sorry for the decision I made to appear as I did in this photo and for the hurt that decision caused then and now. This behavior is not in keeping with who I am today and the values I have fought for throughout my career in the military, in medicine, and in public service. But I want to be clear, I understand how this decision shakes Virginians' faith in that commitment. I recognize that it will take time and serious effort to heal the damage this conduct has caused. I am ready to do that important work. The first step is to offer my sincerest apology and to state my absolute commitment to living up to the expectations Virginians set for me*

when they elected me to be their Governor." –
Ralph Northam, February 1, 2019 via the
Richmond Times-Dispatch

To be fair, nobody's perfect, it's tough to see him in
that photo. I mean it's not like he had a racist nickname
when he attended Virginia Military Institute (VMI). Right?
Right?!? A few days later, a second photo of Ralph emerged.
This photo clearly shows Ralph in his VMI uniform, and is
labeled, *"Ralph Shearer Northam"*. Below his name, are his
nicknames, *"Goose, Coonman"*. Sounds like a real charmer.
Then there's Robert Byrd. He served as a democratic
congressman, and senator at both the state and federal
level for West Virginia. He died in office in 2010. Byrd is
known for filibustering the 1964 Civil Rights Act. He also
recruited over 100 people and founded a whole chapter of
the ku klux klan. He was elected Exalted Cyclops, which is
probably great for a white supremacist to put on their
resume. He to eventually renounced, and told everyone it
was a big mistake. In one interview Byrd is quoted as
saying:

> *"Be sure you avoid the Ku Klux Klan. Don't get
> that albatross around your neck. Once you've
> made that mistake, you inhibit your operations
> in the political arena"* – Robert Byrd, 1997 via
> Wikipedia

His message to others wasn't, "hey kids, avoid racists
groups that have a history of terrorizing American citizens
because they have fundamentally flawed ideologies". No, his
sage advice was a warning to others that basically said
don't join the klan, they won't let you into politics. Not
exactly the most contrite of messages.
Of course, we can't forget George Corley Wallace Jr.
the 45th Governor of Alabama serving for separate four
terms. He too, was life-long democrat. If his name sounds
familiar, he's the fucking idiot that stood in the doorway
refusing to allow the University of Alabama to desegregate.
And if that sounds familiar, there was a Hollywood version

of the scene in the movie, Forrest Gump. But let's go over some of George's greatest hits:

> *"segregation now, segregation tomorrow, segregation forever"* – George Wallace, January 14, 1963 via NPR

> *"I was out-niggered by John Patterson. And I'll tell you here and now, I will never be out-niggered again."* – George Wallace, 1958 via Wikipedia

On three separate occasions he campaigned to receive the democratic nomination for president. Thankfully, he was unsuccessful in his efforts. Not only did George oppose desegregation, he also supported the Jim Crow laws that systematically oppressed black Americans. He was such a turd, that Martin Luther King Jr. referred to Wallace as, *"the most dangerous racist in America"*[3].

Next up is Lyndon Baines Johnson, or LBJ as people usually refer to him. He started his career in politics in 1937 serving the great state of Texas. He was a lifelong democrat and assumed office as president after JFK was assassinated in 1963. He's known for pushing through the 1964 Civil Rights Act after JFK was assassinated. A laudable act. Maybe he was trying to make up for his 20 years spent in congress where, he:

> *"opposed every civil rights bill that came up for a vote, once calling the push for federal legislation a farce and a shame"* – Barack Obama, April 10, 2014 via PolitiFact

If you have trouble believing Barack Obama, maybe you'll believe a direct quote from LBJ himself:

---

[3] As quoted by: https://kinginstitute.stanford.edu/encyclopedia/wallace-george-corley-jr

*"These Negroes, they're getting pretty uppity
these days and that's a problem for us since
they've got something now they never had
before, the political pull to back up their
uppityness. Now we've got to do something
about this, we've got to give them a little
something, just enough to quiet them down, not
enough to make a difference. For if we don't
move at all, then their allies will line up against
us and there'll be no way of stopping them,
we'll lose the filibuster and there'll be no way of
putting a brake on all sorts of wild legislation.
It'll be Reconstruction all over again"* – Lyndon
B. Johnson, via goodreads.com

There is a second, perhaps more notorious quote that is unproven, but is alleged to have occurred in the presence of two U.S. senators. I won't provide it here, but if you're interested you can look it up, and I would say here is one of the rare occasions snopes.com actually provides a fairly good investigation and analysis of a subject. It's also well documented that LBJ was aggressive in his use of the word, nigger, when referring to black Americans.

I could keep going, as the list goes on. I'm sure all this information is in some way shaping your opinion, and it should. These facts have certainly formed and reshaped my views on the Democratic Party as a whole. From my perspective, the Democratic Party is like the hall of fame for white supremacists. They have a deep history of racist policies, and racist ideologies that exist to this day. Gun control is probably democrat's second most polarizing party platform. Gun control is entirely rooted Jim Crow law. The very idea of a gun permit was created to prevent poor minorities, specifically black Americans from being able to defend themselves. It's tough to burn a cross in someone's yard if they're pointing a shotgun at your face while defending their home and their family.

Those facts can be tough to read for some people, and even tougher to accept. But reading is one of the most important skills a person can learn. It will help them throughout their entire life. Reading enables them to learn about our history, and hopefully help them avoid repeating the same mistakes we've made as a community, as a country, and as humans. Reading about and learning from our past also enables people to preserve the (imperfect) institutions that work well. It allows us to also correct the flaws that exist and fill in the gaps some people fall through. For this great sin people are likely labeled a conservative by many of their friends, a republican by many of the people they meet, and a racist by the average liberal democrat. Frankly, society needs conservative values to provide the framework to form a cohesive and stable society. The leftist notion of tearing down American institutions, and smashing capitalism is absurd. But conservatives must also remember that society needs a balanced approach to progressive values, so we don't stagnate or worse, as we face new problems. As the Marines might put it, we need to be capable of adapting to overcome challenges.

For the people who weren't aware of some of the facts and history of the Democratic Party listed above, well, now you know. More knowledge is always a good thing. For the people that are party-line towing liberal Democrat which at this point in history is equivalent to communist, feel free to try and prove me wrong. Go to Google and search all of them. If you're going to do that, I'd also recommend spending some time on Google researching the seven stages of grief. Try not to get stuck in the denial stage. These facts are well documented. How a person interprets them or what lens they choose to view the history of the Democratic Party through is up to them. As with everything in life, what an individual chooses to do with this information is a personal freedom that can never be taken away. I won't tell someone that they're evil for identifying as a democrat. I might poke fun at them a bit, but I'll still get a beer with them, and share a meal with them. I have many friends, from hardcore vegan socialists, to pot smoking hippie communists, and MAGA hat wearing republicans. I would say at some point, those hardcore democrats will need to reconcile what it means to them that the Democratic Party is founded upon the racist ideals of white supremacy. Then they will need to decide whether they believe the Democratic Party has truly changed, or just got better at hiding their racism.

As a personal note it's my opinion (because of my Japanese heritage) the most egregious on the aforementioned list is FDR, who intentionally destroyed Japanese-American families, and their communities. Modern day democrats often cite him as a model for their socialist policies. He is revered by the Democratic Party, and most democrats, and is probably the most celebrated democratic president in history. This is something I was forced to reconcile as I learned more about American history. When I first registered to vote, it was as a member of the Democratic Party. Despite my knowledge of the things FDR had done, I refused to acknowledge them until my mid 20's. In fact, I basically ignored how the Democratic Party had been born of hatred and malice into my early 30's. Then one day I just realized and accepted the fact that being a democrat, and the entire Democratic Party wasn't for me, and probably never would be. This becomes especially burdensome when someone just assumes, I'll be voting democrat because of my racial heritage. Their assumption just feels kind of... racist.

Why did I talk about all the evils perpetrated by the Democratic Party? Partly because they're an easy punching bag right now. I see things like tacit endorsement for rioting and defunding the police and I'm appalled. The libertarian in me absolutely supports massive police reforms including things like mandatory and continuous martial arts training, better and more firearms training and instruction, clearly defined rules for personal accountability, and improved psychological screening. Yeah, it would be a lot of effort, but if we're going to give a person a gun, and the authority to use it against American citizens, there should be a high bar for minimum qualifications. As a U.S. Marine, I was held to a higher standard. I think it's okay to ask at least that same minimum from our police. I think we need to end the war on drugs. It has created a tangle of laws that has given rise to high intensity encounters between police and American citizens that continue to escalate and are clearly a recipe for disaster. With all that said, I also consider my father, and my friends that own small businesses. I don't get inspired by a political party that would openly support burning their shops down because a handful of union protected cops are poorly trained, psychopathic, racist piles of shit. Part of me hopes the democrats will actually get their shit together, but then I remember they openly support marxists ideas and hope they all take long walks off a short observation deck 100 floors up.

I also wanted to talk about the horrific past of the Democratic Party because many people are simply not aware of their history. That's because it's just not talked about, and not taught in school, and that control of information is really what this book is about. How could the American people know if they were never taught? What if that information was simply censored, deleted from the history books altogether? All throughout history there have been attempts by those in power to horde knowledge and keep it away from the people they feel entitled to rule. It's tied directly to modern political ideologies such as fascism, but ultimately, it's a common theme across human history: controlling others. It's the same reason that education for slaves became illegal in the United States, and sadly, society is experiencing another cycle of it. Only this time it's worse. New technology has allowed mass media outlets to achieve a level of influence never before experienced and it's led to biased editorial decision making, intentionally deceptive journalism (let's call that what it is, propaganda), and the selective censorship of conservative, and minority voices. This censorship is growing and is an existential threat to a free society. It's the most widespread use of social gaslighting ever seen and it's being perpetrated by a single-minded group of individuals. These disinformants have the ability to directly influence what, and how news stories are to be sold by corporate news media. They control what messages and ideas big tech firms will allow to be said or seen by their millions of users. This disinformation campaign occurring because the voices, perspectives, and opinions that are being silenced have been deemed dangerous knowledge.

chapter 2: the trump effect

Don't misunderstand my dumping on the Democratic Party. The Republican Party has its fair share of misdeeds, bad actors, racists, misogynists, homophobes, and outright egregious authoritarian policies (the war on drugs comes to mind). We don't need to cover those in this book. We all know about them. We hear about every mistake, misstep, and misdeed any conservative politician or conservative voice will make. The glossed up, narrative approved story will make our 24 hour a day news cycle until the next conservative voice or Republican politician makes a mistake. The story will be trending on Twitter with all the predictable, and fashionable tropes. Each one carefully crafted and designed to end with one singular conclusion: orange man bad. It'll be in everyone's Facebook news feed as all the people we knew in high school post why it was the "end of humanity as we know it!!! OMG!!". Or why it was the, "best thing ever #MAGA". It'll be front page news on every corporate media website and shoved in our faces on every corporate media TV channel. Say the line: orange man bad.

Journalism is no longer acting as society's referee. Instead they seem to have built a divisive circus act populated by angry clowns. This is how journalism works now. After all these are private companies and were never under any obligation to remain neutral. What's concerning to me is how much control corporate media has over information. CNN, Fox, MSNBC, CBS, etc., and now big tech Google, Facebook, Twitter, Instagram, etc., specifically social media platforms use this control to silence dissent. These companies are controlling what information a person can see, and what a person can say on a massive scale. Primarily this is done because certain facts or talking points don't match the narrative being fostered by that company. Maybe it's me holding on to the ideals of freedom of speech, freedom of thought and attempting to apply those ideals to a private company. They aren't bound to those same rules of fair play. Despite how ubiquitous it has become; Google remains a private company. By private company I mean not a public utility or service such as the DMV or courthouse. Yes, I am aware that Google is a publicly traded corporation. Maybe I had become too comfortable with the notion that Google held to its motto: *"don't be evil"*. Maybe I believed their technology platform was truly unbiased and provided the best search results for what I was browsing the internet for. Maybe this was never true, and they've always pushed their own leftist agenda, slowly manipulating all of us. Maybe I'm just being paranoid. These thoughts are frustrating for me and I think they became disturbing as I sit writing this during the ongoing pandemic, during the waning days of the 2020 election cycle.

This trend to control information accelerated rapidly during the 2016 election cycle. Or maybe I just became more aware of it. Either way when Donald Trump threw his hat in the ring to seek the Republican nomination for president in 2016 the wheels started to come off for journalism, and society at large. It was the first step towards the genesis of a disease that has been termed, Trump Derangement Syndrome or TDS. TDS is characterized by a negative reaction to anything and everything President Trump does or says regardless of the quantitative good or bad of whatever he said or did. TDS began to spread slowly amongst liberals, and even some conservatives, when the Trump 2016 campaign launched. And the more traction Donald Trump gained, the faster it spread. The better Trump performed in the polls, the more the American public heard how evil his: family, friends, associates, neighbors, business partners, buildings, golf resorts, name, hair, skin tone, money, jet, companies, books, socks, food choices, basically anything he did was bad, racist, misogynist, and terrible. If his ties had feet, they would kick puppies!! It was (is) ridiculous and it all became an echo chamber for virtue signaling how good a person you were.

Question: do you hate President Trump if yes > acceptable; else > cancelled. How do I know this? Because we were told this. By CNN, by MSNBC, by CBS, by Twitter, by Facebook, by Hillary Clinton, by Nancy Pelosi, by Cenk Uygur, by Rachel Maddow, and all the other talking heads. Trump supporters are:

> *"You know, to just be grossly generalistic, you could put half of Trump's supporters into what I call the basket of deplorables. Right? The racist, sexist, homophobic, xenophobic, Islamophobic, you name it."* Hillary Clinton, September 9, 2016 via Time.com

So, starting in 2016 and through 2020 at least, making sure President Trump is taken down became the only thing that mattered. I'm assuming President Trump will win reelection this coming November, which he will. And when he does, corporate media platforms can't (and won't) just end their propaganda machine so this behaviour will probably extend through 2024 as well and probably beyond. People were so sold on this moral gatekeeper question a 'Never Trump' coalition of establishment Republicans was formed. They seemed to gained traction for a time. In fact, most established Republicans were on the fence when it came to Trump, for a while. It was a wait and see strategy for them. They were trying to assess how the public would receive such a polarizing politician that had a knack for making off the cuff remarks. What they ignored was President Trump's ability to connect with people frustrated by 8 years of divisive democratic policies that seemed to leave them behind.

Were any of them wrong? Donald Trump's detractors or Donald Trump's supporters? Maybe. Maybe not. Some people might ask, "how could they not be? There are so many experts who say Trump is...." It's a fair point, and a valid question from both perspectives. Everyone should answer that for themself and formulate a clear opinion they can articulate. Once they have done so, I would be more than willing to get together, drink a beer or two, and we can have a reasonable discussion about our opinions, how we came to them, and some of the finer points of a Trump presidency. Again, pontificating on President Trump's successes (he's had a few) and failures (he's also had a few) isn't really the point of this book. People will try to argue that he's the most evil person ever, and nothing he's done has been good, or they will try to tow the opposite line and say he's a saint, sent by God, to deliver God's own words. It's probably not either of those things so you need to get over whatever deep seeded ideas that were indoctrinated into you from whichever corporate news channel.

Very few things in this world are 100% good (puppies) or 100% bad (sweet pickles, they're gross, and basically just alien turds). President Trump is no exception. Despite all his success he's probably somewhere in the mix with the rest of us. He has his strengths, his weaknesses, and it's not for me to judge or assign him some quantitative value of his goodness or badness in life because I just don't know that much about the man. I know more about the democratic bad actors I listed in the previous chapter because I've spent the last 10 years or so trying to reconcile my journey from a naive California democrat, to a resentful republican, to a frustrated libertarian, and now to mostly just a fed-up America. I feel confident in my analysis that the people I mentioned earlier led terrible lives, however I'll probably never meet any of them. I've also never met President Trump, and don't expect I ever will. Don Jr. seems nice, as we both enjoy hunting and fishing. From his Instagram it seems he's far more successful than me at both and I admire people who are good and successful at things I enjoy doing. Yet I also don't know Don Jr. so it's just as likely he's a complete prick.

The most I know about President Trump is that he managed to raise at least one kid that likes to hunt and fish (like me), he was on Lifestyles of the Rich and Famous when I was growing up, and he's really good at making democrats very angry about quite literally everything. But those angry people are the same ones who thought Ellen was the nicest person on the planet. Based on recent events half of Ellen's staff can't stand her. So, I think I'll leave the determination of the goodness and badness of someone I don't know much about up to the fiction writers over at the Good Place. The broader point is less about what I do and do not know about President Trump, but more than I refuse to believe the corporate media narratives the orange man bad gang is pushing. When corporate media only shows the public the moments when a person is at their worst, the image they've built is less than flattering. It's no different for President Trump. The manner in which CNN, FoxNews, MSNBC, Twitter, Facebook, reddit, and so many others build up a public persona is nothing short of social engineering. And for the past 4 years corporate media on the left has been devising and implementing hundreds of ways to sell the narrative that orange man bad. In short, they've been gaslighting America.

As a result of that gaslighting, the orange man bad gang has unwittingly given President Trump an interesting power. Rather than tear him down, President Trump now has the ability to incite visceral, emotionally charged reactions from liberal democrats. Ironically, these visceral reactions provide hours of entertainment for President Trump's supporters. The crying, the screaming, every video posted to Twitter, Instagram, and Facebook forever immortalized into meme form by conservatives. It's been entertaining to watch the entire situation. All the angry reactions, and abhorrent behaviour that President Trump seems uniquely capable of inciting in most of these leftist corporate media journalists (propaganda ministers).

Liberals seem both enamored by and infuriated with President Trump. It's how I know Trump Derangement Syndrome is real. Love him or hate him, it should be indisputable that President Trump has done a few things very well. Prior to the covid-19, I guess we're calling it a pandemic, the economy was booming. In a recent report it's noted that the poverty rate for 2019 declined 0.8 percent from 2018, and median household income rose 4.5 percent. This represented one of the sharpest year to year declines in poverty since 2005, and an indicator that President Trump's economic policies seemed to be working. I'm sure there are some economists and couch bound quarterbacks out there saying any of the following: it wouldn't have lasted, it was built on a lie, all it did was benefit billionaires, or it was Obama's economy. To them I say, it all rolls up. But I guess we'll never know because using their infinite wisdom, democratic governors, and mayors tanked the economy with draconian, unconstitutional lockdowns denying American citizens of their most basic rights. Including the right to work and feed themselves.

How good was Trump's economy? So good the democrats tried to take credit for it. On February 17th, Barack Obama sent out the following tweet which was accompanied by a picture I won't include:

> *"Eleven years ago today, near the bottom of the worst recession in generations, I signed the Recovery Act, paving the way for more than a decade of economic growth and the longest streak of job creation in American history." -* @barrackobama, February 17, 2020

That's a laughable statement, and here's where we're going to wade into TDS, before jumping headfirst into some of the more absurd things the orange man bad gang has said and done in order to push the orange man bad narrative. Even though we'll go over some of those absurd stories, they're less nefarious than the first example precisely because they're so absurd. This example is more subtle, and a far more insidious version of TDS. So, let's take some time to parse out and untangle what narrative the liberal media is pushing. There are three different stories linked together here with the same goal in mind: orange man bad. It's like liberal journalists are compelled to try and prove that nothing President Trump does can be good. To begin our journey, here's a quote from an article published by CNN:

> *"Just how bad would it get? The downturn under a President Trump would last longer than the Great Recession. About 3.5 million Americans would lose their jobs, unemployment would jump back to 7%, home prices would fall, and the stock market would*

plummet, Moody's predicts." - Heather Long,
June 21, 2016 via CNN

Scary. Quite a doom and gloom prediction by CNN.
Separately, in an article published by Reuters:

*"Nearly half the U.S. counties carried by
President Donald Trump in the 2016 election
were arguably in recession at the time, with
local economic output shrinking during a
campaign that focused on the declining
fortunes of blue-collar America."* - Howard
Schneider, December 18, 2019, via Reuters

The implication being the reason 'Trump Country' was
'Trump Country' is this economic recession, and that
President Trump was able to exploit it by leveraging the
economic downturn into a 2016 victory.

Clearly, the article published by CNN turned out to
be a completely false prediction. The fact that a journalist
was willing to make such dire claims should be disturbing
to everyone. Their attempt to use fear with sensationalized
headlines, and influence an election isn't good citizenship,
and it certainly isn't good journalism. It's not even close to
bad journalism, it's propaganda and can be dismissed as
such. That still leaves a couple scenarios. If the Reuter's
article is true, and we are to believe Barack Obama as he
claims 11 years of economic growth in his tweet, then his
policies also mean leaving behind much of blue collar
America, and leaving many people who lived in those
depressed areas to suffer. This would also mean President
Trump's economic policies truly did help the people living in
those areas left out and ignored by Obama's globalist
democratic strategy, and President Trump should be given
credit for helping to improve people's lives. But this runs
contrary to the dictum: orange man bad.

If the Reuter's article is not true, then President
Trump won those counties because the people there simply
rejected Democratic policy from the past 8 years and
embraced Trump's America First promises, which again,

would run contrary to the dictum: orange man bad. And either way, if a person loves President Trump or hates the man, it would mean one of two things. Either his policies were effective at improving the economy for the people experiencing economic downturn, or he's good at engaging people with charm and charisma, much like Obama and Bill Clinton were. If it's the former, Obama's tweet is absurd. If it's the latter, then the Reuter's article is a hack piece designed to undermine President Trump because orange man bad. And to all the President Trump fans out there, it would be a mistake to underestimate either Barry or Bill for their charm and charisma.

This news thread and many more like it, do lead to questions on what defines journalism, and do professional journalists have a responsibility or ethical code to follow? Is it all just the will of whatever publisher they work for? While pondering these questions, the term journalistic integrity comes to mind. For the record, there's an entire Wikipedia page devoted to journalism ethics and it provides the set of five values broadly accepted as a code of ethics for journalists quoted here:

1. ***Honesty:*** *journalists must be truthful. It is unacceptable to report information known to be false, or report facts in a misleading way to give a wrong impression.*

2. ***Independence and objectivity:*** *journalists should avoid topics in which they have a financial or personal interest that would provide them a particular benefit in the subject matter, as that interest may introduce bias into their reporting, or give the impression of such bias. In cases where a journalist may have a specific financial or personal interest, the interest should be disclosed.*

3. ***Fairness:*** *journalists must present facts with impartiality and neutrality, presenting other*

*viewpoints and sides to a story where these
exist. It is unacceptable to slant facts.*

4. **Diligence:** *a journalist should gather and
present pertinent facts to provide a good
understanding of the subject reported.*

5. **Accountability:** *a journalist must be
accountable for their work, prepared to accept
criticism and consequences.*

Again, this list was from Wikipedia[4]. I am by no
means a professional journalist. When answering my
questions from earlier, in the context of the guidelines I just
listed, it probably depends on who a writer works for. In
today's fast paced world and 24-hour news cycle it must be
tough to operate a functional and profitable news media
company. The advent of the internet, and the dearth of
independent and crowd sourced news has hastened the
decline of print media and has made people desperate. In a
span of around 20 years, an industry generating over $65
billion dollars shrunk to less than $20 billion. Did this
downward pressure contribute to the complete
abandonment of these core values? It probably didn't help.
No matter which political party a person aligns themself
with they likely read the journalism values list and laughed
at least one of the major cable television news networks.
I've met three types of people when it comes to cable news:
people who think FoxNews is about as fair and balanced as
a dumpster fire, people who think CNN is the Ministry of
Propaganda for the Democratic Party, and people who think
both channels are trash heaps.

The derangement in Trump Derangement Syndrome
comes from its apparent ability to cause journalists to
completely disregard and abandon any or all 5 of those core
values in the name of greater good. After all, orange man
bad. But it's not just journalists. Political pundits, sports

---

[4] As quoted by:
https://en.wikipedia.org/wiki/Journalism_ethics_and_standards

athletes, comedians, actors, basically any category of person with a tie to mass media has at least one well-known figure that has completely abandoned reason when it comes to President Trump.

> **Derangement** - *the state of being completely unable to think clearly or behave in a controlled way, especially because of mental illness.* – the Cambridge Dictionary, September 2020

For example, Rosie O'Donnell and President Trump have famously feuded on twitter for over a decade, and a Trump presidency wouldn't end it. The spat started in 2006 over a disagreement about some of the things Rosie said about then Mr. Trump. Her claims of bankruptcy are alleged to have been what upset him as they were untrue, unfounded, and because he had various business partners, and investors, a false claim of bankruptcy could have had real world consequences for those investor relationships. He fired back his response, and the rest is history. During the 2016 election cycle the things he had said to and about Rosie O'Donnell were brought up during one of the Republican debates.

I think it was supposed to be a gotcha moment. The moment that finally ended the circus that had been a Trump presidential campaign. The moderator, Megyn Kelly would ask her questions, and Trump would be trapped, forced to give an unpopular answer and people would boo him out of the 2016 election. I don't think anybody, not even the early and fervent Trump supporters were prepared for his answer. About halfway through Megyn's question regarding some of the past comments Trump had made, he interjected with, *"only Rosie O'Donnell"*[5], to which the crowd cheered raucously. Megyn Kelly tried to remain composed and finish her question but the gravity in the room had shifted completely and the only one that seemed to know which way was up, was Donald Trump. He allowed her to finish her question appearing thoughtful, then gave another

---

[5] President Donald Trump, August 6, 2015 via FoxNews

response garnering even more raucous applause, and that was that. The moment to end Trump 2016 had evaporated.

This moment was also the final nail, driven into the coffin of ethical journalism, confirming its death until at least 2024. That question, Trump's response, and the crowd's reaction that night, in front of thousands of people, being broadcast to millions of homes across the country cemented the strategy of how corporate media would deal with Donald Trump. The gloves were to come off, there were to be no more rules, and certainly no guiding principles. Trump couldn't be defeated by playing fairly, and from then on, in the minds of liberal journalists everywhere, Trump needed to be defeated at any cost. I think those journalists have consistently underestimated, and undervalued what the true costs are, and the long-term impact the decision to abandon all boundaries is having. Not in just how it's redefined journalism over the past 4 years, but how that decision has reshaped politics into a toxic, and divisive game of real or imagined gotcha moments.

So how does that all relate to our exploration of TDS? Let's start with this headline, tweeted out by then Newsweek reporter Jessica Kwong:

"How Did Trump Spend Thanksgiving?
Tweeting, Golfing and more" -
@JessicaGKwong, November 28, 2019

The tweet links to a story published by Newsweek discussing President Trump's activities for Thanksgiving. Seems reasonable to report on the activities of America's president, on one of America's national holidays. The trouble is that the story was completely false (see section 1 of the journalism values). President Trump was actually taking a trip to Afghanistan to visit the troops deployed there supporting the Afghan people. The president served food, shook hands, and by all accounts it was a great trip and a nice moral boost for the troops by our Commander-in-Chief. I'm not certain if the author had a bad source that completely misinformed them, or they completely fabricated the story, but the author's response to being caught was a second tweet later that day. In their reply they write:

> *"Trump headed to Afghanistan to surprise U.S. troops on Thanksgiving (...) Deleting this tweet because it was written before knowing about the president's surprise visit to Afghanistan-an honest mistake. Story has already been updated, as shown in the screenshot." -* @JessicaGKwong, November 28, 2019

Maybe it was an honest mistake. A simple lapse of diligence described by the values of journalism. We all make mistakes. But was it an honest mistake? The author could have stated they had been misled by a normally reliable source, or a normally reliable source had been mistaken, and apologized for rushing to publication. Those would be reasonable explanations as to how a journalist had been so completely wrong. They did none of those things, and simply called it a mistake. Maybe it's wrong but is it unreasonable to think a professional journalist should give a more detailed explanation? I'm not claiming they should make a bunch of excuses or attempt to deflect but maybe just explain what happened. X, Y and Z happened, or I rushed the story, or I didn't double check my sources, and my story was incorrect. I apologize. We all move on. Ultimately the author was fired by Newsweek which I don't necessarily think was the right decision unless they had willfully fabricated the story. The only person who will ever truly know how that story came to be is the writer. I mention it now because it is an example of how a journalist didn't really care about the potential consequences of writing a false story if that story supported the narrative, orange man bad. This callous disregard for the professional consequences a journalist might be faced with by engaging in such behaviour shows a lack of clear decision making.

Jump to December 20, 2018. A story broke about a reporter who had fabricated a series of published stories. One MarketWatch headline read:

"CNN 'Journalist of the Year' peddles fake story about Trump's America, resigns" - Shawn Langlois, December 20, 2018, via MarketWatch

The article describes how Claas Relotius, the CNN journalist of the year, had completely fabricated much of the content for a series of articles they had submitted to their publisher. The series was about 'Trump Country' and the people who lived there. It was such an egregious offense that Der Spiegel's (where the fabricated articles were published) top editor Ullrich Fichtner had this to say:

> *"The truth [is] that his sources were anything but clear. Indeed, it is likely that much of it was made up. Inventions. Lies. Quotes, places, scenes, characters: All fake."* - Ullrich Fichtner, December 20, 2018 via MarketWatch

By any measure that is a damning statement in an industry where the number one value is alleged to be honesty. The author claims their slip in morals was driven by a fear of failure, and pressure to succeed. Possibly, but why did they think they could get away with such a clear violation of ethical norms? Is it because he felt attacking President Trump was a slam dunk? Nobody would disbelieve his stories, after all, as we all know Trumpers are a basket of deplorables. Again, the only person who will truly know their intent is the writer. And again, it's another journalist engaging in behaviours they normally wouldn't while promoting the narrative, orange man bad.

May 2017. A picture of comedian Kathy Griffin holding a severed, bloody head resembling President Trump gets posted on the internet. It goes viral. She was not prepared for the controversy her photo created. In a fading career as a comedian, and having been a part of a reality television show, Griffin probably thought it would garner her some publicity from the orange man bad gang. Release the photo and everyone would applaud in unison. The crowd would shout, "say the line" as she parroted back, "orange man bad!!" Cue snare drum, that's the show folks. What actually happened was the complete crash of her career. Currently she's still struggling to make it back into the spotlight as it appears, she's still suffering the consequences of that fateful decision.

After the photo was released, there was immediate backlash and condemnation from conservatives, leading CNN to fire her. She claims she was also blacklisted in Hollywood, unable to find work. She claims she was put on the no-fly list for a couple months while federal agents investigated her photo as a direct threat to President Trump. Federal law makes any credible threat a federal felony (United States Code Title 18, Section 871). She claims the photo was from an unscheduled shoot she agreed to do last minute. It was between gigs and she just thought it would be a funny political statement. Certainly, a believable story. That's probably half true. There was probably a part of her thinking, "fuck this mother fucker" that she is leaving out. Regardless it's another behaviour symptomatic of TDS. With liberals in the country still reeling from shock over a Trump victory (it's 2020 and the left is still reeling from shock) the previous November, President Trump was an easy liberal punching bag for some publicity and a laugh. There was that stretch of time when every comedian was doing bits about Trump. It became tiresome. A lot of people really thought they could say anything to bash President Trump and get a laugh, or career, out of it. Some people have made Trump bashing a career. Griffin is not one of those people.

On June 2, 2017 Griffin gave a press conference. It was not an apology this time, it was more attacks against President Trump, blaming him and his family for ruining her life. *"He broke me. He broke me. He broke me"*[6] Cue the tears. I don't think she should have been fired for trying to make an unfunny joke. Sometimes comedians write a bit and it just doesn't hit. It happens. But sometimes we make decisions that have long lasting impacts. This was one of them for Kathy. Audiences can be fickle, and if you're in the

---

[6] Kathy Griffin, June 2, 2017 via CBS News

entertainment business the crowd can and will turn on you at some point in your career. Regardless of the outcome, I'm reminded of the definition of derangement. Not able to think clearly or behave in a controlled way. Maybe. Maybe not. I feel like this situation was more that a comedian felt there was no line they couldn't cross when it came to attacking President Trump. The deplorables thought otherwise. That's what makes it TDS. The boundlessness of a person's decision making when weighing the impact of a decision to attack President Trump in a particular fashion. There's no consideration for the consequences, because there generally aren't any.

As of 2020 Griffin still seems bitter about the entire situation. While First Lady Melania Trump was giving her speech during the broadcast of the 2020 RNC, the former comedian had this to say:

"Seriously, fuck this bitch." - @kathygriffin,
August 25, 2020

Strong words. She tweeted more things about President Trump's family, but I couldn't tell if they were jokes from her new special or not because of how derivative and unfunny they were. Griffin wasn't the only celebrity tweeting about First Lady Melania Trump that night. Bette Midler jumped into the fray and tweeted this about the First Lady:

*"Why are they promoting this awful person,
#melania? Was it in her contract? She says it
feels like just yesterday they were at their first
convention. Maybe to you, Mel. For the rest of
us every day has been a horrible slog thru the
9th Circle of Hell. #beBust"* - @bettemidler,
August 25, 2020

Not the worst attack our First Lady has needed to endure from the orange man bad gang. Midler followed up her initial insult and hurled this xenophobic tweet:

"Oh, God. She still can't speak English." -
@bettemidler, August 25, 2020

Yikes. Not a good look for a ride or die liberal. One twitter user called her out, and wrote this in response:

> *"When Liberals are so bad that you have to defend Melania Trump. This is beyond gross @BetteMidler and I am no fan of the First Lady. You have become what you think you are "resisting.""* -@ProudSocialist, August 26, 2020

After some backlash from all sides, Midler later tweeted her apology for her comment:

> *"Well, all hell has broken loose because I said Melania "still can't speak English" last night. I was wrong to make fun of her accent. America is made up people who speak with all kinds of accents, and they are all welcomed always."* -@bettemidler, August 25, 2020

Maybe it's that for the past 50 years she's been an elite celebrity living with extreme wealth and power. I have a friend who says, *"power doesn't corrupt, power magnifies."* I tend to believe them. But to Midler's credit she did apologize because all hell broke loose. So, I guess she wouldn't have apologized otherwise? Unclear, but this is just another example of the orange man bad gang willing to say anything, true or not, to hurt President Trump and his family. The boundlessness of the behaviour is what makes it another example of TDS.

These types of insults are not the only instances when the orange man bad gang engaged in questionable behaviour regarding the First Lady. In February 2017, the New York Times was forced to admit one of their reporters was spreading unsubstantiated rumors that First Lady Melania Trump was a hooker. An article posted at TheWrap.com reported that the NY Times was forced to admit through a spokesman that this rumor spreading was a mistake and that:

> *"the comment was not intended to be public,*
> *but it was nonetheless completely*
> *inappropriate and should not have occurred." -*
> NY Times, February 13, 2017, via theWrap

Really the story itself wouldn't have been a story if not for actress Emily Ratajkowski having the courage, and integrity to speak up, and call out the New York Times in a tweet.

This was an active decision by someone who represented the New York Times that didn't go as expected. Their decision making as a journalist reflects questionable ethics at best. Going back to the list of journalism values, a journalist who would knowingly spread unsubstantiated rumor clearly isn't acting within the bounds of professional conduct. Again, this crosses into TDS territory due to the willingness of this person to cross those boundaries of ethical journalism with no regard to the potential repercussions. Not only did this journalist undermine their own integrity, but they've also added to the growing pile of intentionally deceptive practices eroding the trust in news media as an industry, and journalism at large.

When 'not my president' became a clarion call for the orange man bad gang shortly after President Trump was elected, conservatives chuckled. To this day it's a running joke in my circle. But for the orange man bad gang, it's no joke. There's a Facebook page titled Not My President that identifies as a political group targeting President Trump. As of August 2020, this group had nearly 750,000 likes. For comparison, democrat Joe Biden's official Facebook page has around 2.5 million, Hillary Clinton's page has around 9.8 million, and President Trump has nearly 29 million. In an opinion piece posted at the WashingtonExaminer.com commentator Erich Reimer had this to say:

> *"a March University of Chicago poll showed 57*
> *percent of young people believe Trump is an*

illegitimate president." - Erich Reimer, April 28, 2017 via the Washington Examiner

While Reimer clearly disagrees with this sentiment, he does give credit to members of the Democratic Party later in the article by noting that:

"Clinton, President Obama, and many other Democrats attended President Trump's Inauguration and emphasized that, while they were unhappy with the result and would continue to resist the president, they accepted his legitimacy." - Erich Reimer, April 28, 2017 via the Washington Examiner

It is a bit pedantic to claim individuals touting the, 'not my president' motto mean and believe the saying literally. Despite their disappointment, frustration, and other expressive behaviours regarding the election of President Trump I would imagine of the roughly 750,000 people following the Not My President Facebook page only a small fringe element believes the words literally. The motto is more of a rallying cry, a virtue signal to others that yes, they too are card carrying members of the orange man bad gang.

This is confirmed by the organizers of the 'Not My Presidents Day' rallies against President Trump. These rallies, in various cities, were held on Presidents' Day in 2017. Organizers made it clear that yes, President Trump was duly elected, but the 'Not My President' was a political statement that President Trump did not represent American values. This is exactly why the first amendment exists, how the first amendment is supposed to work and I laude them for exercising that right. They peaceably assembled, to protest their perceived grievances against their elected government.

But exercising the first amendment is not how this political movement got started. It started when Green Party presidential nominee Dr. Jill Stein demanded a recount in three states that traditionally voted democrat but had turned red during the 2016 election. In December of 2016 Stein held a press conference in front of Trump Tower in New York and had this to say:

> *"We're here today to stand up for a vote that is accurate, secure, fair and just, in which every vote counts"* – Jill Stein, December 5, 2016 via the Guardian

By this point around $7 million dollars had been raised to fund her recount efforts in these three states: Pennsylvania, Michigan, and Wisconsin.

Those efforts largely failed. Federal judges in Pennsylvania, and Michigan stopped the recount. However, in Wisconsin, the Clinton campaign joined Stein's efforts and after some legal maneuvering, the Stein campaign paid a $3.5 million dollar fee, and a recount was ordered to begin on December 1, 2016. After a week and a half, and more lawsuits, the Wisconsin vote recount was finished. The results? President Trump had increased his win margin by 131 votes.

A few other states performed recounts independent of any party demands and only minor vote tally changes occurred. Overall, it had been a huge waste of time and resources. Dr. Stein's own running mate Dr. Ajamu Baraka had openly opposed the recount efforts. He stated in a Facebook post that:

> *"The recount effort has resulted in serious questions regarding the motivations of the recount that threatens to damage the standing and reputation of the Green Party, its supporters and activists"* - Dr. Ajamu Baraka, November 28, 2019 via Facebook

Dr. Baraka was correct. Dr. Stein hadn't just demanded a recount to ensure the integrity of the election and protect voters. During her recount efforts she had made a few inflammatory claims about the election results. Here's a statement released by Dr. Stein in defense of those efforts:

> *"After a bitter, divisive election, now facing*
> *serious threats to our civil and constitutional*
> *rights, defending the bedrock of democracy -*
> *our right to vote, and to be confident in that*
> *vote - is more important than ever."* – Jill Stein,
> 2016 via Jill2016.com

After a Pennsylvania state judge denied her initial request for a recount, Jill Stein made the following statement:

> *"It's clear that the fix was in against a verified*
> *vote in the state of Pennsylvania, so we are*
> *now moving to a federal court to ask the court*
> *to please stand up for our constitutional right to*
> *vote."* Jill Stein, December 5, 2016 via the
> Guardian

Not only is she saying the election results were wrong, but implying that a state judge, in good standing, was a part of the conspiracy to give President Trump a victory. Dr. Stein also made claims that votes from some Michigan precincts were missing. Even though she had no evidence to support either of her claims, Dr. Stein was willing to undermine the entire democratic process of our country based upon one ideology: orange man bad.

In her mind President Trump was so bad that it would be worth the cost to sow discord, discontent, and divisiveness across the nation. During the election campaign, a now iconic picture of a person holding a sign that says, *"It's not rigged you're just losing"* and sporting a, "MY VOTE IS FOR HILLARY" shirt. The person has a big grin, as they pose for the photo op. At the time Hillary was predicted to win by almost every pundit, poll, and expert that just knew Hillary was going to win in a landslide. When the shoe switched feet, the messaging followed it seems. Rather than stand by their principles, the orange man bad gang abandoned their stance of, *"it's not rigged, you're just losing"* and switched to *"the fix was in"*. Again, it's less that they switched positions, it's the manner in which it was done. There was a complete lack of evidence that widespread voter fraud, or conspiracy had occurred to hand President Trump a victory. Yet here we were, enduring a month of reckless accusations from a group of bitter individuals, willing to go to any length, say anything true or not, to undermine President Trump.

Question: If President Trump is so terrible, so bad for America, such a wretched soul, why would anyone need to misrepresent the things he does or says? All the examples in this chapter, the fake stories, the false rumors, the hateful attacks, the undermining of our very democracy, why? Why all the effort? Because orange man bad? Okay. But we live in a democracy. Shouldn't people, right or wrong, be free to make their own choice about who they want for president? It's really fucking patronizing that the orange man bad gang believes they have the right to dictate how and who a person should vote for because of their own political leanings. That's called tyranny, and that's what a person engages in when they try to harass, berate, belittle, someone else for voting for President Trump. When a journalist allows TDS to justify abusing their role as a trusted source of information, by deception or other means, those actions turn them from respectable citizens, to nothing more than stewards of fascism.

No matter how terrible the orange man bad gang thinks or feels President Trump is, people are free to vote for him and don't need permission or approval from anyone but themselves. It is also a person's right to nominate, and vote for a presidential candidate they feel is better than President Trump. Maybe by their standard, that's a can of tuna fish. Instead of trying to control how other people vote or think, they should try to nominate a candidate that appeals to more than a narrow, fringe segment of society.

What truly defines TDS for me is when a person is willing to cross their own personal boundaries in the name of some perceived greater good. Because no matter how bad a president, or presidential candidate is, when a person crosses the moral boundaries they have established for themselves, and go on to use orange man bad as justification for those indiscretions, that is a stain on their soul that will never come off. And if a person has no moral boundaries when it comes to 'resisting' President Trump, perhaps they should take a long look in the mirror and decide what that says about them as a human.

chapter 3: down the YouTubes

The Trump effect, and TDS were the catalysts that justified a clamp down on information by authoritarian leftists. Even though most people might have seen the ongoing battle of misleading news and reporting by traditional media sources, the biggest influence TDS has had is in the digital marketplace and so we'll begin there, with YouTube. YouTube, founded in 2005 as a video sharing platform, it was purchased in 2006 by Google for $1.65 billion dollars. In 2019 it had an annual revenue of $15 billion. One of the ways it derives revenue is through ads before, during, and between video plays. People can go onto YouTube and watch official music videos published by their favorite musicians. They can watch stupid cat videos, funny clips of people doing various things, videos of people fighting, videos of people making cakes, or painting their fingernails or cutting hair. Per stats from Wikipedia, and as of 2020, over 500 hours of content are uploaded to YouTube every minute, and over 1 billion hours of content are watched every day worldwide.

A part of YouTube's revenue is derived from selling ad space between, and during the videos posted on their platform. What has helped make YouTube so successful is the part of their business model that shares some of that revenue. Meaning content creators who gain a certain number of followers and views are eligible to participate in a program where they can receive a portion of revenue generated by YouTube. Once creators opt into this program, and they meet all the requirements, they will be able to earn income depending on the popularity of their content. I don't know how YouTube payment models or ad models work but I'm sure as an advertiser you would have the option of buying ad space on specific types of videos, or specific channels of content. After all targeted ads is one of the things the internet is known for and where some of the competitive advantage lies.

So being able to monetize a YouTube channel essentially means anyone is able to start and produce their own television show. The program is called the YouTube Partner Program. What is the YouTube Partner Program? From Google's own description:

> *"The YouTube Partner Program (YPP) gives creators greater access to YouTube resources and features."* - Google

To qualify for the YPP there are some minimum requirements, and some community guidelines which I will list here:

1. *Spam, deceptive practices, and scams*
2. *Nudity and sexual content*
3. *Child safety*
4. *Harmful or dangerous content*
5. *Hate speech*
6. *Harassment and cyberbullying*

At face value, these rules seem pretty reasonable. A bit of quality and content control to keep out the riff raff. Also, because they are a private company, they retain the right to say what types of content will be allowed to use the platform they have created to generate revenue. And in this regard, YouTube goes further with stipulations on any content related to firearms which create extremely strict guidelines on what is and is not acceptable for participation in the YPP program. Again, it is their right as a private company. What happens if a person were to violate these policies? Well YouTube, and it's incredibly wise, and unbiased referees (insert eyeroll) have the answer:

> *"If your content violates this policy, we'll remove the content and send you an email to let you know. If this is your first time violating our Community Guidelines, you'll get a warning with no penalty to your channel. If it's not, we'll issue a strike against your channel. If you get 3 strikes, your channel will be terminated."* - Google

Again, these policies seem pretty fair in concept thus far. I've never thought about making any content to put on YouTube or monetizing it. If that ever changed, I would feel confident that YouTube would be equitable in their enforcement of their own policies. That confidence may be misplaced, as an article published on Ammoland.com caught my eye. In the article, the author opens strong with the following two sentences:

> *"Google has once again struck out against Second Amendment channels on its YouTube video sharing platform. The tech giant has set out to demonetize channels dealing with guns even if the creators do not violate YouTube's terms of service."* - John Crump, July 16, 2019 via Ammoland

That second sentence was what put me on notice that my assumptions of fair play by YouTube may have been premature. Even if they, *"...do not violate..."* the terms of service? Then what's the point of the terms of service? Isn't that breach of contract? False advertising by breaking an official offer? Agree to these terms, post content, and the content creator will earn a share of the ad revenue YouTube sells. That was YouTube's promise. These were all the thoughts that came to me as I continued to read.

As it turns out, YouTube had begun demonetizing gun instructional videos as a political statement months earlier. Accordingly, they also began updating their community standards to match their gun control virtue signaling. YouTube had added stricter rules for what was and was not allowed. Again, this is their right as a private company, and Google's CEO and therefore Google, and YouTube have taken a strict gun control stance to appease liberal democrats in Silicon Valley. There are a couple of troubling aspects to how these rules are applied. The first problem I see is that content creators are not being notified by any form of communication that they were no longer eligible to participate in the YPP, and their channel would be demonetized. This is a violation of YouTube's own stated policy (see above). The second problem I thought of was not only is YouTube demonetizing channels for vaguely violating the community standard with no communication, explanation, or the 3 strikes they talk about, they had also begun demonetizing channels simply discussing guns and debating the 2nd amendment. John Crump (the article's author) claims his channel was demonetized for what he was told was, *"posting harmful content"*. And it's that second piece that just does feel right.

Regardless of where you stand on the issue of gun control in the U.S., people should be free and willing to have thoughtful, impassioned debates about their varying opinions. Political discourse is the very soul of America. It defines the very notions of freedom of speech and freedom of thought. Thoughtful discussion and rigorous debate are not harmful. In fact, debate is the opposite of harmful, it is helpful. It is helpful in shaping opinions, it is helpful informing the uninformed, and it is helpful in creating dialogue between parties that may have been previously at an impasse. Why would YouTube find discussion harmful? The only reason I can think that someone would find debate or opinion sharing harmful is if they were attempting to control the opinions of another person by controlling their access to information. A truly democratic society should believe in the agency of the individual, and any attempt to shape that agency through deception or by controlling information or differing opinions would be an act of tyranny. But that couldn't be it. That seems somehow evil, and Google's code of conduct clearly states, *"don't be evil"*.

People should be free to agree or disagree with a particular political opinion after hearing the arguments laid out. What would it mean if they never get to hear those arguments? What if all they were allowed to hear is one side of the debate, one opinion, or one perspective? How would that influence their decision making? Here's a bigger question: what if you could control what information people were allowed to see? How would you use that influence? What if it was your company that could control what types of opinions and information could be shared? How would your company use the ability to manipulate and control what people see?

Let's circle back. Earlier I listed YouTube's community standards. Number four addressed harmful or dangerous content. Number five addressed hate speech. Again, these two rules, or rule categories seem pretty reasonable at face value. I'm sure most people's minds went immediately to, "well yeah, we don't want the white supremacists on their recruiting people and espousing their hateful beliefs, and we probably shouldn't show people how to make bombs. These are good rules." I make that claim with some air of confidence because that was my initial reaction. Then I reminded myself knowledge is never harmful, and as a mathematician (turned writer apparently) knowledge for knowledge's sake is a good thing. Evil people can certainly take knowledge and use it for evil purposes, but the information simply existing is not harmful.

This proposition led me to another thought: some of the things that I would find useful, would actually be extremely harmful for someone else. For example, instructions on how to TIG weld around a pipe flange. I have a basic understanding for how a wire-feed welder operates, and the associated safety precautions. However, someone with no experience welding might: burn themselves, blind themselves, electrocute themselves, asphyxiate themselves, burn down a building, or worse. A person experiencing any of those outcomes would highly likely be extremely harmed. Therefore, I propose that all videos containing instructions on advanced TIG welding techniques be taken down for violating YouTube's community standards. Or is that not the spirit or intent of the community standards? Let's be practical here, that would probably not meet the spirit or the intent of the rule. I'm sure nobody at YouTube was thinking the rules should be interpreted literally. YouTube probably meant (and this is pure speculation) let's not allow users to upload videos of people demonstrating how to make a bomb with household chemicals. There may be unintended consequences that cannot be taken back. These guidelines were probably developed early on at YouTube and when they formalized rules, they were probably just designed around liability issues that the YouTube legal advisors suggested.

However now that this analysis has been performed, and a reasonable person can conclude there's a general intent to each of the community standards. That does however leave us wondering, what is YouTube's intent behind demonetizing channels that debate political issues or present opinions? John Crump claimed his channel was simply posting videos of people discussing the 2nd amendment. What is the intent of banning or demonetizing a channel that only posts gun reviews where a content creator uploads discussions about a lawfully obtained, and legally owned firearm, what they like, and dislike about it? I think these are fair questions. Is it to keep people safe from harm? What harm is there in open debate or opinion-based evaluations? Would that harm be supporting the 2nd amendment? This is where YouTube is venturing into territory that makes me uneasy. The control of information because the left simply doesn't like it.

Again, I support YouTube's right as a private company to allow or disallow whatever content they see fit. However I would remind the readers here that YouTube has made a formal offer, posted it publicly, that creators abided by when generating and posting content, that YouTube is continuing to profit off of, that is surreptitiously demonetized. Wouldn't it be easier to simply say they don't support the 2nd amendment and they won't allow any of that content on their website? All the deception, the attempts to control, stigmatize, or manipulate, what people can or cannot advocate for, all that effort to mislead seem a bit evil.

Support for the 2nd amendment wasn't YouTube's only target they went after to control people's opinions. Conservative commentator Steven Crowder had his channel demonetized. The YouTube support team provided the following statement regarding the issue:

> *"[YouTube] came to this decision because a pattern of egregious actions has harmed the broader community and is against our YouTube*

> *Partner Program policies"* – YouTube, June 5,
> 2019

A little more than a year later in August of 2020, YouTube announced Crowder's channel would be allowed to rejoin the YPP and begin generating ad revenue once more. What's interesting about this case is that the day before YouTube decided to demonetize Crowder's channel, they publicly announced that Crowder's channel and the content it contained didn't violate their policies. Why the extra scrutiny? Was YouTube seeking to punish a conservative voice? Or did Crowder truly step over the line. Regardless, the outrage mob activated, and the very next day, he was cancelled. In responding to the demonetization, Crowder seemed unphased, and certainly unapologetic to the mob. He gave a few statements but claimed he really didn't generate much revenue from YouTube and made more money from other segments of his business.

If this had been an isolated incident that was controversial simply because his content had toed the line a little too closely this would be a blip in the YouTube story. However, Crowder hasn't been the only overtly conservative voice targeted (rightly or wrongly). PragerU was also targeted for what their legal team has generally referred to as conservative censorship. As early as 2017 they filed suit against Google-YouTube for violating their first amendment rights, which hey, it's their money. The lawsuit went about as far as you might think: a private company (non-government) has no obligation to protect a user's first amendment rights, because as the judges correctly asserted YouTube is not a state actor. Even though Prager-U had their day in court and lost, there were a couple of interesting things about the Prager-U complaint. The first were items 55 and 56 from the complaint. Prager-U alleged YouTube had responded to an inquiry (email) regarding restricted flagging sent on September 21, 2016 with the following:

> *"As mentioned in the previous emails, at this
> time, your videos aren't appropriate for the*

younger audiences and hence they're not appearing in the restricted mode search results. I'd recommend you to go through our Community Guidelines and align them with your content to see where it has violated." – Prager University vs. Google Inc, October 23, 2017 via Case 5:17-cv-06064-LHK

Curious. The second was a listing of videos the Prager-U legal team assembled as evidence for their lawsuit that allegedly demonstrated biased enforcement of YouTube community standards. In this list they had named 32 videos, highlighted in red that had apparently been categorized by YouTube as age restricted based on the statement provided by YouTube. What is age restricted content? According to YouTube from their help center:

Sometimes content doesn't violate our policies, but may not be appropriate for all audiences. In these cases, our review team will place an age restriction on the video, or remove the thumbnail, when we're notified of the content.

Age-restricted videos are not visible to users who are logged out, are under 18 years of age, or have Restricted Mode enabled.

What will result in an age-restriction? Here are some of the things we consider for age-restriction:

1. *Vulgar language*
2. *Violence and disturbing imagery*
3. *Nudity and sexually suggestive content*
4. *Portrayal of harmful or dangerous activities*

If you believe we made a mistake, you can appeal the age restriction.

> *Monetization and age-restrictions*
> *If you're eligible to monetize, make sure you*
> *review our policies. Age-restricted videos are*
> *not eligible for monetization and are not shown*
> *in certain sections of YouTube. Age-restricted*
> *videos are also not eligible to be used as ads.*

Just like YouTube's other guidelines and standards, these seem pretty straight forward at face value. I wanted to check this out for myself, as I don't think I had ever experienced age restriction on YouTube before. Honestly it took some effort to find even one video that was self-flagged as age restricted. Using the incognito mode on my web browser (I use Opera) I navigated to YouTube and searched for a specific video I knew to be age restricted from a tutorial video I had watched a few moments earlier. Incognito mode is a mode on your browser that keeps you hidden and deletes all the browser history when the window closes. It also means I wouldn't be logged into my Google account when arriving at YouTube and would be unable to view age restricted content without logging in first. Sure enough, the age restriction was working, and I was unable to view the specific video I had found that had been self-flagged by the uploader. I then began the tedious task of copying and pasting each of the video links Prager-U had listed in their lawsuit against YouTube as being age-restricted.

Prager-U's primary complaint regarding the video list was that they had been flagged by YouTube moderators, but other videos with similar content, topics of discussion, or general subject matter had not been flagged by YouTube. Prager-U felt this indicated YouTube was unfairly targeting them because of their conservative political stances and opinions. It's a valid concern. I would think the community standards would be applied equitably to all content creators. The Prager-U v. Google-YouTube lawsuit was from 2017 (Case 5:17-cv-06064-LHK) and as I worked my way down the list, none of the videos came back flagged. I only made it about halfway down before giving up. This had been a dead end, or dead issue. Either way, YouTube seemed to be on the up and up in this instance.

Or was it? Three years had passed since the lawsuit had been filed so I began digging a little deeper to see if maybe somehow Google's algorithms had defeated my anonymity and really knew who I was (apparently it had I later discovered). No dice. I did some more searching (really all this only took about 30 minutes of effort). This led me to a website called The Christian Post and an article titled, *YouTube blocks PragerU Ten Commandments videos, restricts to 'mature audiences'*, provided screenshot evidence of YouTube flagging two out of six videos previewed in the screenshot as being flagged. This made me wonder if those were still censored. I opened a new window in opera, this time just a regular browser, tracking, history, cookies and all. I navigated to YouTube where I was immediately recognized and logged into my account. I turned ON my restricted filter, and there they were. Little grey boxes wearing frowny faces. On a playlist provided by the Prager-U channel titled, *Religion / Philosophy*, eight out of the thirty videos are nothing more than those little grey boxes, wearing the little frowny faces. When I tried to click on them, I was given the YouTube message indicating that the content I was attempting to view had been flagged restricted. Why? They must meet one of the criteria listed by YouTube. Vulgar language, have violent or disturbing imagery, have nudity or sexually suggestive content, or portray harmful or dangerous activities. So, I unrestricted my account, and began watching.

First up on the list was (at the time) number 11 - Are Humans More Valuable Than Animals? Odd question, but let's do this. At a brief 5:49 minutes what could it hurt? First let me say there was no vulgar language, there was no nudity or anything sexually suggestive, and there were no harmful or dangerous activities. The only imagery provided was some animations matching the narration, and narrator speaking. The narrator (Dennis Prager) opened by talking about the Judeo-Christian belief that humans were created in God's image and therefore human life was sacred. He also gave an alternative opinion that if humans were just composed of matter, and with no God the creator involved, that would mean human life is indifferentiable from other matter, and therefore human life was no longer sacred.

I am not a religious person by any means. I won't make the standard, "I'm not religious, I'm spiritual" as some folks do, trying to hedge. I would be best described as a skeptical agnostic. I won't get into a religious debate here, but I will say that after watching this I really see no reason for this video to be restricted. The only thing that might have gotten the video flagged was when it mentioned a PETA exhibit that had equated eating meat to the holocaust. It didn't show any imagery from the exhibit, only mentioned it as a negative outcome if human life is not treated as sacred. Really it didn't meet any of the four criteria YouTube has provided.

Next up was a video titled, *The Ten Commandments: What You Should Know*. As a nonreligious person it was tough to sit through because I have no interest in religion. However, unless boring is a restrictable category, there's really no reason for this video to be flagged either. Now I was becoming curious as to why these videos were flagged. What was so dangerous about them? How did they not meet age restriction requirements? I started digging around more and discovered there were actually two types of categories that can flag a video: age restricted, or just restricted. Age restricted standards are the four content restrictions listed earlier in the chapter. As it turns out restricted videos have a much broader definition I'll quote here:

> *Videos containing potentially adult content will not be shown to viewers who have Restricted Mode turned on.*
>
> 1. ***Drugs and alcohol:*** *Talking about drug use or abuse, or drinking alcohol in videos.*
>
> 2. ***Sexual situations:*** *Overly detailed conversations about or depictions of sex*

or sexual activity. Some educational, straightforward content about sexual education, affection, or identity may be included in Restricted Mode, as well as kissing or affection that's not overly sexualized or the focal point of the video.

3. **Violence:** *Graphic descriptions of violence, violent acts, natural disasters and tragedies, or even violence in the news.*

4. **Mature subjects:** *Videos that cover specific details about events related to terrorism, war, crime, and political conflicts that resulted in death or serious injury, even if no graphic imagery is shown.*

5. **Profane and mature language:** *Inappropriate language, including profanity.*

6. **Incendiary and demeaning content:** *Video content that is gratuitously incendiary, inflammatory, or demeaning towards an individual or group.*

We know there's a risk that some important content could be lost if we were to apply these rules without context. We value stories where individuals discuss their personal experiences and share their emotions. Sharing stories about facing discrimination, opening up about your sexuality, and confronting and overcoming discrimination is what makes YouTube great, and we'll work to make sure those stories are included in Restricted Mode. But just a reminder, to be included, your content must follow the guidelines above!

I wasn't quite back to square one. I think I see why YouTube was flagging at least the first video as restricted content. Section 4, mature subjects. Specifically, political conflicts that resulted in death or severe injury. During the video debating human / animal life, it mentions the fact that both Nazi Germany and the Communist Parties in Russia and China began labeling people they murdered as 'sub-human' or 'party enemies'. These were (and are) political parties that would use animal comparisons for the 'undesirables' as justification for murder. But the video didn't provide specific details. It was thin, so I went back to YouTube once again and searched for channels with videos that may or may not be flagged restricted, but not age restricted.

As luck would have it, I found a channel called Simple History. The entirety of its content is animated, and they have several videos discussing, as you probably guessed, historical topics. I remained on the channel's home page, made a brief mental inventory of the videos, before clicking on my restricted mode filter. Honestly I didn't see much of a change, I scrolled down a bit and saw a video (with restricted mode ON) titled, *How Long did a Person Stay Alive after being Guillotined?*, that was posted on November 26, 2019 and had garnered almost 8 million views when I clicked on it. The first 15 seconds or so was a soft open with severed human heads on pikes, with one being animated to match the narrator speaking.

I'm probably the least squeamish person I know. I hunt and have cleaned and butchered wild game in the past so I'm fairly unphased by this time of imagery. The next scene opened with an animated person's head being chopped off in a guillotine. I clicked on another video titled, *The Catherine Wheel - Worst Punishments In The History of Mankind,* from the same channel. Again, everything was animated but this video showed depictions of people being tortured and discussed various ways in how they were murdered. Both videos appear to meet the standard of graphic descriptions of violence.

Both videos I watched from Simple History were posted in 2019. Yet they weren't flagged by YouTube, and I don't think they should be. However, in order to be consistent in the application of its rules, and as a subsidiary of Google, be consistent with the Congressional testimony given under oath by Google CEO Sundar Pichai in December of 2018, then these videos should be flagged as restricted content. Further, if YouTube was truly only flagging the Prager-U content because of the general restricted content guidelines, then why would YouTube's response specifically mention younger audiences? While their message quoted early doesn't explicitly state Prager-U was flagged as age restricted, the phrasing is intentionally misleading. It's this type of behaviour that calls into question YouTube's intent. Google CEO Sundar Pichai has stated that:

> *"I lead this company without political bias and work to ensure that our products continue to operate that way. To do otherwise would go against our core principles and our business interests. We are a company that provides platforms for diverse perspectives and opinions and we have no shortage of them among our own employees"* - Sundar Pichai, December 10, 2018 via CNBC transcript

If we are to believe Mr. Pichai, then I have to question why the Prager-U videos are flagged restricted, and the Simple History videos are not. Both appear to be violating the community standards set forth by YouTube, both discuss violent activities perpetrated in the past as a part of human history. Why does there appear to be a different standard of enforcement of the content rules for Prager-U, a well-documented conservative voice, as compared to Simple History which I would imagine (and genuinely seems) to be apolitical? Why does YouTube seem oriented around controlling what information conservative voices are allowed to share with the public? I'll leave those questions for everyone to decide for themselves.

chapter 4: the twitterverse

Leslie D'Monte called it, the *"SMS of the internet"* in her 2013 article published by business-standard.com. With the rise of Twitter, some people might start to call SMS, private tweeting. Regardless of the collective opinions on the usefulness of a tweet, and the company called Twitter, it's ubiquity as a communication tool is undeniable. Even if a person doesn't have a twitter account, almost everyone knows what Twitter is. If you don't know what Twitter is, imagine a giant message board indexed by people rather than topic, and all the messages they post are 280 characters or less. It was a simple idea, but here are some quick stats taken from Twitter's Wikipedia page:

> *"Twitter was created by Jack Dorsey, Noah Glass, Biz Stone, and Evan Williams in March 2006 and launched in July of that year. By 2012, more than 100 million users posted 340 million tweets a day, and the service handled an average of 1.6 billion search queries per day."* - Wikipedia, September 5, 2020

In 2019 Twitter reported revenue of $3.46 billion dollars, claimed over 300 million users, and owned subsidiary companies Vine, Periscope, and Mopub. Not bad for a company founded on the idea of inconsequential information. Tweets have ruined careers, created great moments in comedy, elevated people who previously didn't have a voice, and ignited political firestorms, all in less than 140 characters (in 2017 Twitter doubled the character limit to 280). In chapter two I mentioned liberal democrats providing play by play analysis of certain RNC speeches. Why would someone do this? So they can show everyone how virtuous they are. If orange man bad, then showing contempt for orange man clearly demonstrates how much goodness a person has in them (eye roll). In Twitter terms, those people are looking for likes, replies, and retweets. For the social media industry, those likes, replies, and retweets are interactions that constitute the term referred to as reach.

Reach is a metric used to sum up how many followers, and interactions a social media personality has. It's basically how much popularity that social media account has, as a quantified measure. Traditional celebrity status can be measured by things like box office ticket sales, television ratings, or jersey sales. Social media personality, including more traditional celebrities, have far more precise metrics available to them, due to the data tracking algorithms and statistical tools companies like Twitter provide. The more popularity a Twitter account has, the more reach a person such as Bette Midler has. This translates into more money that person can make selling ad space or tweets for companies paying for them. In fact, right now, there are people you've never heard of, selling social media posts, making thousands of dollars, because they have a social media reach companies find valuable. Those people are called influencers. Advertisers like influencers because they have a broad audience that can be directly marketed to.

And so, Twitter became increasingly popular, and more mainstream, traditional holders of influence began creating Twitter accounts to interact directly with their fans and supporters. As this happened, more and more less savory people realized they could impersonate, or misrepresent other people or entities. Imagine how someone could shift the stock market if you controlled an account that claimed to be Barack Obama. If enough people followed such an account while he was president and sent a tweet that announced a moratorium on all fossil fuel use in the United States it would have a huge impact. Stock market would tumble, oil prices would crash. It might be enough to trigger a global recession. It is a nightmare scenario that has thus far remained fiction.

That fictional scenario was something that Twitter hadn't thought of or considered enough of a problem to solve. Afterall, how could someone from 2006 predict that by 2012, half of society would be tied to their phones, furiously tapping their screens arguing with their friends while sitting on the toilet? But as Twitter gained traction, and became increasingly popular, there were a number of well-known celebrities who complained about the fake, parody, and impersonated accounts that proliferated across the platform. Even though these fake accounts had much milder consequences than the scenario described earlier, not many people enjoy being misrepresented. Twitter was becoming increasingly aware of the issue, but to this point, nobody had taken legal action to force Twitter's hand. In fact, it took until 2009 after a series of Tweets made by an account impersonating baseball legend Tony La Russa for someone to seek legal relief. Mr. La Russa took exception to this, and early in 2009 filed a lawsuit against Twitter. Little known fact, Tony La Russa has his JD from Florida State University. Eventually after some talks Tony requested the lawsuit be dismissed, but the event did spur a response from Twitter, and they decided to take action. That summer, Twitter launched a test version for their verification program, and what would eventually become the blue check mark.

A blue check mark serves to indicate to other Twitter users and followers, that the account owner is accurately represented by the account name. More or less, if the account has the Twitter blue check mark, and claims to be Barack Obama, then that is actually Barack Obama's Twitter account. This was a turning point for Twitter, and really allowed the company to expand. In Q1 of 2010, 6 months after the launch of the blue checkmark, Twitter had an estimated total of 30 million active users. By Q1 of 2012, Twitter had grown to 138 million active users. Until the launch of their blue check mark, Twitter had been hamstrung by people creating fake accounts to impersonate and misrepresent celebrities. With the blue check mark though, advertisers could now be certain it was Kanye West sending out tweets to his 30 million (as of August 2020) followers. While this led to the problem of hacked accounts, overall, it seemed to create a better experience for Twitter's user base, and the numbers show this.

As Twitter began to grow, it became increasingly mainstream as a communication tool for reaching large audiences. Twitter played a central role as a communication channel for politicians and pundits alike. By August 2018 it was considered one of the largest and most important digital battlegrounds for political discourse for liberal and conservative voices alike. That's why it was shocking when conservative voice and political commentator Candace Owens posted an inflammatory tweet:

> *"Jewish people are bullshit… like dogs pissing on fire hydrants. #cancelJewishpeople. Are Jewish people genetically disposed to burn faster in the sun?"* - @RealCandaceO, August 4, 2018

Clearly the ravings of an anti-Semitic hate monger who deserves to be silenced. Twitter agreed and @RealCandaceO was promptly banned, blue check mark and all. The only problem was what she had written below that message:

> *"The above statements are from @nytimes editor @sarahjeong. I simply swapped out the word "white" for "Jewish"* - @RealCandaceO, August 4, 2018

No problem, Twitter will simply ban this Sarah Jeong person for posting clearly hateful, racist rhetoric. Honest mistake. Only Twitter didn't do that either. Twitter didn't respond by banning the individual responsible for the racist comments, they apologized for banning the person who identified the racism. Wait, what? For clarity I'll interject here that I don't support banning people for exercising free speech. I like knowing that racists are allowed to clearly identify themselves with the racist comments and ideologies they harbor, and not hide in anonymity. What I don't understand is how a mechanism implemented by Twitter designed to catch content that violates Twitter's rules only caught one offender, and not the other, and further why Twitter didn't address Sarah Jeong's tweets at the time.

Thankfully, when Candace Owens was suspended, she was able to find support from fellow conservatives and was grudgingly reinstated. After the suspension, she released an email response from Twitter:

> *"Twitter takes reports of violations of the Twitter Rules very seriously. After reviewing your account, it looks like we made an error."* - Twitter, August 5, 2018

Just an error. Still, shouldn't Twitter enforce their standards for content regardless of who violates them? Their statement still doesn't explain why Sarah Jeong wasn't banned unless Twitter is also making the claim this type of overt racism isn't a bannable offense. Which may be the case and is consistent with the continued support for racist, dehumanizing tweets made by the correct people. In October of 2018 Louis Farrakhan tweeted:

> *"I'm not an anti-Semite. I'm anti-Termite"* - @LouisFarrakhan October 16, 2018

As an update, Farrakhan's tweet has since been deleted as Twitter updated their rules in June of 2019. Only then was Louis's account suspended until he deleted those tweets. It took 9 months.

Perhaps it'll make more sense if I explain who Sarah Jeong is. At the time she was recently hired as a New York Times editor, with a law degree from Harvard, and author of the book, *The Internet of Garbage*. She also tweeted the following wholesome messages:

> *"Dumbass fucking white people marking up the internet with their opinions like dogs pissing on fire hydrants"* - @sarahjeong, November 28, 2014

> *"#CancelWhitePeople"* - @sarahjeong, November 18, 2014

"1) white men are bullshit 2) no one cares about women 3) you can threaten anyone on the internet except cops" - @sarahjeong, December 31, 2014

"oh man it's kind of sick how much joy I get out of being cruel to old white men" - @sarajeong, July 24, 2014

For those people who are waiting for me to explain why it was acceptable for Sarah to make horrible racist comments on Twitter, documenting her racist beliefs, established in a clear pattern of behaviour, you'll be waiting a long time.

Luckily, her new employer, the New York Times, quickly came to Sarah's defense. After all, how would it look if a company that describes itself as dedicated to making the world more just for everyone was caught hiring someone who had been exposed for making racist comments openly and publicly? Surely, they had exculpatory evidence demonstrating that these tweets were not representative of Sarah's character, and the reason behind the tweets. On the topic, they had this to say: she was joking. I'm paraphrasing but that's what it came down to. Their defense of Sarah Jeong was that her tweets were clearly regrettable satire posted in response to online harassment. As a person who has been the target for racist harassment throughout my professional career I can tell you these are the same excuses HR directors have given me about the terrible directors and managers I've been forced to endure. "He is bad with words" or "he has poor communication skills" or "she didn't mean it like that" is the hallmark of a toxic workplace with a problem they don't care to fix.

The problem I have with the defense the New York Times provided is that Sarah's profession is writing, and she posted most of these thoughts as what appear to be standalone tweets (though I could be wrong) rather than replies to very real, very sick comments intended to harass her. In reality the only question that really matters at the end of the day is if you believe Sarah Jeong is a racist in her heart. In my opinion Sarah answered that with her own words, and I would challenge each individual to answer that question for themselves.

Candace Owens hasn't been the only victim of liberal tech companies wielding fascist like authority to control information and stifle people's ability to make informed decisions. A feminist journalist named Meghan Murphy was also banned from Twitter. "Ah ha," the leftists exclaim, "see, feminism is a core tenet of progressive, liberal ideology, clearly there is no bias at Twitter". That is half true. The banner of feminism is carried proudly by the orange man bad gang, wearing their pink pussy hats and waving their, "it's not rigged, you're just losing" signs. But ideological purity tests are the hallmark of the Democratic Party, and Meghan Murphy ran afoul of those communist ideals.

Make no mistake, Murphy is a self-avowed liberal. She believes the gender wage gap exists, and that women are systematically discriminated against, supports socialism, and abortion rights. She supports the #metoo movement, has argued against allowing male feminists to guide the feminist conversation, argued against the porn industry as exploitative and misogynistic, and was extremely critical of Hugh Hefner when he died. Yet Murphy also believes in free speech and free thought, and the benefits of rigorous debate. So much so that despite her opinions she also opposed the Canadian bill C-16 that eventually became law. In her opposition to this proposed law, she was invited to give testimony before Canadian Senate where she stated:

> *"Treating gender as though it is either internal or a personal choice is dangerous and completely misunderstands how and why women are oppressed under patriarchy as a class of people"* - Meghan Murphy, May 10, 2017

This was the beginning of the fracture between Murphy and the mainstream feminists, and mainstream liberals.

Though her statements were more about the codification of what she, and other intellectuals felt was compelled speech, she wasn't towing the party line. In an interview with Simon Shepherd broadcast on News Hub Nation, Murphy stated:

> *"I don't believe that it's possible to change biological sex. So I think that you're born either male or female, and you remain male or female for life. So I disagree with the idea that you can identify as female if you're male. I also, of course, have concerns about gender identity legislation and policies and the way that they impact women, and particularly women's spaces where women and girls might be particularly vulnerable, so change rooms, transition houses, prisons."* - Meghan Murphy, November 15, 2019

Her beliefs on transgenderism and feminism didn't align with mainstream feminism and so she became persona non grata. Murphy is what those holding leftist ideals refer to as a terf or trans exclusionary radical feminist. What does that mean? Good question. A terf is an individual who rejects the idea that a person who identifies as a transgender woman is the same as a biological woman.

It's these beliefs that got her banned from Twitter. Not just generally thinking them but standing by her beliefs in several posts on Twitter's platform. The tweets in question? One of Murphy's tweets that drew the ire of the inner party was this:

> *"@CiriAntares @joandark11 @Sara_Rose_G @tavarish_ @petefrasermusic men aren't women tho"* - @MeghanEMurphy (now banned), October 11, 2018

Kind of a tautology, regardless of your opinion on the trans community isn't it? Without getting too deep into logic, if a transwoman is a woman, then she has no need for the trans qualifier, and it stands that, yes, men are not women.

But this statement, and logic, runs counter to the purity test established by liberal gatekeepers, and so Murphy was forced to delete the tweet. Then, at some point during this saga, Murphy tweeted, *"Yeeeah it's him. https://[...]"*. This was the only piece I could find, which was a screen shot posted by another twitter user, Graham Linehan on November 25, 2018. In the screen shot, Murphy was told her account was suspended, and eventually permanently banned for violating the rule against hateful conduct. The conduct in question? Murphy had misgendered the Canadian national known as J. Yaniv. This was the individual that was caught on video tape appearing to physically assault, and curse at a journalist. The reason for the apparent assault? The journalist had been waiting outside of a courtroom where Yaniv was facing charges on possession of a prohibited weapon.

But there we have it. The viewpoint that transwomen are not women is verboten by liberals. It's wrongthink. It's thoughtcrime. I won't debate the trans person narratives here, again the broader concern is that ideas and voices that don't fall in line with liberal ideologies are being removed from public discourse. I don't share Murphy's ideas about socialism. I believe socialism is a sick and deadly ideology that has murdered over 100 million people. But if Murphy thinks starving 40 million people to death in Maoist China was a good idea that just needs some tweaking, she should be free to discuss that. She should also be free to discuss, promote, and share any of her opinions with others to drive thoughtful engagement and discourse. This includes her ideas, opinions, and thoughts about transgenderism and its role in a feminist movement. Afterall, she is a woman with the genes to prove it.

"Well Meghan Murphy is Canadian," someone might say, "and that country doesn't have the same freedom of speech protections that the United States." After all, Canada is a part of the British Commonwealth and they're throwing people in jail for Facebook memes, and arresting pregnant women for organizing rallies against corona lockdowns. So, Twitter must have just been making sure Meghan didn't get thrown in jail for saying disagreeable things. It's a kindness really. That's a fair point I suppose. Let's explore that a little because it would mean Twitter should explain how, in July 2018, several Republican congressional representatives had their Twitter accounts suppressed. They did explain, and according to Twitter, this occurred because of a change to an algorithm. Allegedly this change was intended to target 'bad-faith actors'. When this occurred, because those bad-faith accounts were engaging with the Republican party congressional reps, all their accounts were flagged. Flagged for what? Flagged to be shadow banned.

Shadow banning is a practice social media companies engage in when they are attempting to silence a user without the user realizing it. Different from other forms of disciplinary actions which are explicit, a person usually won't even realize they're being punished. While Twitter disputes these actions being regarded as shadow bans, if you were to Google the term, the very first definition, of about 100 million results is from Wikipedia which states:

> *"Shadow banning, also called stealth banning, ghost banning or comment ghosting, is the act of blocking or partially blocking a user or their content from an online community so that it will not be readily apparent to the user that they have been banned."* - Wikipedia, September 10, 2020

That's pretty much exactly what Twitter did regardless of how much Twitter wants to wordsmith their own definition of the term. Even if this shadowban was intentional or not, it's tough to deny the result. The most galling part of their scripted denial was that Twitter had already admitted this shadowban was intentional. In May 2018 they were beginning to suppress Twitter users who didn't violate their terms of service. Why would Twitter want to suppress people who didn't break any rules? After all, they claim they advocate for:

"for free expression and protecting the health of the public conversation around the world." – Twitter, September 2020

That's a direct quote from the company, and there seems to be some minor inconsistencies there. Twitter claims that these bad faith actors are, *"harmful to healthy conversation"* should indicate to them that they need to update their terms of service to stop these harmful behaviours. Wouldn't that make more sense if these alleged behaviours were truly harmful? Twitter intentionally opted for a shadowban approach. Was it intended to be a tool with a broader intent? Possibly.

If it's a shadowban, and the user isn't supposed to know, how was it discovered? A team working with republican Matt Gaetz' noticed a drastic change in their metrics around May 15, 2018. Data provided by the Gaetz team showed about a 10% reduction in overall impressions, and about half as many new followers once Twitter began their shadow ban campaign. Vice News then broke the story on July 25, 2018 and reported that, *"prominent conservatives aligned with President Trump"* were no longer being included as recommendations when searching for them directly. Vice went even further, performing similar searches for the entire Progressive Caucus appeared normal as Twitter's auto-populate feature recommended leftists such as Maxine Waters, Keith Ellison, and Tom Perez.

No matter how it was discovered, the victims of Twitter's ongoing conservative harassment included: U.S. Representative Matt Gaetz of Florida's 1st district, U.S. Representative Jim Jordan of Ohio's 4th district, and former U.S. Representative, and current White House Chief of Staff Mark Meadows. These individuals are (or were at the time of the shadow ban) duly elected public officials. They were elected to represent the voice of the citizens in their districts. Surely, because of who they represent, more than anyone should be allowed to speak up and speak out for those voices using a forum created by a company that claims to be, *"committed to protecting freedom of expression."* Representative Matt Gaetz had this to say in an interview with The Hill:

> *"I feel victimized and violated by a platform that holds itself out to be a public forum. It's really frustrating to think that the marketplace of ideas couldn't accommodate the thoughts and musings that I contribute."* - Matt Gaetz, July 25, 2018 via the Hill

That's exactly what Republican Party Chairwoman Ronna McDaniel thought. In a statement given to Vice she says:

> *"The notion that social media companies would suppress certain political points of view should concern every American. Twitter owes the public answers to what's really going on."* - Ronna McDaniel, July 25, 2018 via Vice

Ronna McDaniel was also a victim of Twitter's targeted shadow ban. While not an elected official, she raised a good question. What is really going on? Twitter's response to Vice:

> *"We are aware that some accounts are not automatically populating in our search box and shipping a change to address this."* - Twitter, July 25, 2018 via Vice

A non-answer, and so Vice pressed Twitter further by asking why only conservatives were impacted by these algorithm changes. Twitter's response:

> *"I'd emphasize that our technology is based on account *behavior* not the content of Tweets"* - Twitter, July 25, 2018 via Vice

Allegedly. It became such a hot button issue that Twitter released an official statement through Product Lead Kayvon Beykpour in a series of tweets:

> *"To be clear, our behavioral ranking doesn't make judgements based on political views or the substance of tweets. We recently publicly testified to Congress on this topic"* - @kayvz, July 25, 2018

> *"On 2) Some accounts weren't being auto-suggested even when people were searching for their specific name. Our usage of the behavior signals within search was causing this to happen & making search results seem inaccurate. We're making a change today that will improve this."* - @kayvz, July 25, 2018

The behaviour in question? According to Twitter they were attempting to filter out 'troll-like behaviours'. This raises another question: is Twitter calling conservative opinions troll-like? That's really the implication isn't it? Reading through the quotes, non-responses, and waffling statements given by Twitter, it certainly appears that Twitter has implied that conservative voices are: harmful to conversation, troll-like, and unhealthy to public conversation. This is the sanctimonious attitude liberal democrats project that makes it reasonable to assume Twitter is willfully engaging in behaviour that is opposite of advocating for free expression.

Despite all of Twitter's denials, there's video evidence these shadow bans are very real, and very targeted. Project Veritas broke this story through investigative journalism and brave whistleblowers stepping forward willing to capture statements from Twitter employees on video. Their mission, as stated on their website is to:

> *"Investigate and expose corruption, dishonesty, self-dealing, waste, fraud, and other misconduct in both public and private*

institutions in order to achieve a more ethical and transparent society." - Project Veritas, September 2020

What did their investigation discover? In an undercover video obtained by Project Veritas, a former Twitter software engineer Abhinav Vadrevu is recorded saying:

"One strategy is to shadow ban so that you have ultimate control. The idea of a shadow ban is that you ban someone but they don't know they've been banned, because they keep posting, but no one sees their content." - Abhinav Vadrevu, January 3, 2018 via Project Veritas

For those wondering, Twitter had disputed the use of the term shadow ban, and yet a Twitter software engineer was captured on video tape stating this practice was (or still is) one of the tools Twitter uses. Project Veritas has more evidence of Twitter's political bias, this time they captured Mo Norai, a former content review agent at twitter. Mo says this:

"…you know you're looking at it and you're like, oh, hey, this is pro-Trump, I don't like it." - Mo Norai, May 16, 2017 via Project Veritas

This statement was in response to a question regarding flagged content. It was a part of a series of questions to Mo on how content could be banned from Twitter. Further, when questions about the decision making for removing content Mo had this to say:

"A lot of unwritten rules, and being that we're in San Francisco, we're in California, very liberal, a very blue state. You had to be, I mean as a company you can't really say it because it would make you look bad, but behind closed

doors are lots of rules. Like hey, you gotta do this this way, or something like that. It was never written, it was more said." - Mo Norai, May 16, 2017

Not exactly a smoking gun, but a warm shell casing at least. The implication here was that content espousing liberal ideologies were given a pass and pro-Trump ideologies were banned, not for violating rules, but because the people making that decision just didn't like President Trump. Need more explicit proof? How about Twitter engineer Pranay Singh. He was, or is, a direct messaging engineer for twitter. He was asked if Twitter mostly got rid of conservatives. His response, *"yeah."* For those wanting to learn more I highly recommend watching the full report, posted at Project Veritas. While none of these individuals directly state that Twitter has explicitly taken a stance to eliminate conservative voices, it is clear that on some integral level Twitter is attempting to control what information people can, and cannot see by eliminating conservative thoughts, ideas, and opinions from public consumption. In a society that values the notion that people should be heard, ideas shared, and solutions debated, this control of information has a chilling effect.

With over 84 million followers, there should be no doubt in anyone's mind that President Trump leverages Twitter to communicate directly with the American people, and the world. Good. A president should be able to communicate directly with the people they lead. While I disagree with President Trump on a few key policy issues, a few key decisions, and a few rough comments, I appreciate his direct approach with the American people. After decades of living in a world where politicians were expected to give sanitized, lifeless speeches I find it refreshing, even if that means his words are sometimes disagreeable. In the way that Deadpool's R rating changed comic movies, I'm hopeful that President Trump's direct, and honest approach changes the way politicians serve the public.

I also know it's a style not suited for everyone. Just like I love crispy bacon, or a good rare steak, there are some vegans out there that enjoy mushy cucumber slices with a glass of tepid water. Good for them. I probably wouldn't get dinner with them because I really don't need them to tell me how terrible it is to eat bacon or steak. Thankfully, I have the ability to ignore those people because they're about as fun as a wet blanket. President Trump found out in July 2019 as a public servant he is not allowed to just ignore those types of people. At least not on Twitter. A federal appeals court upheld a previous ruling, claiming that because President Trump uses Twitter to conduct government business, it elevates his account to an official, state-run account. Keep in mind it's the same official account President Trump used while he was a private citizen.

In their unanimous ruling, the 2nd U.S. Circuit Court of Appeals stated that President Trump cannot block Twitter users from his official account as it would be a practice considered discriminatory. President Trump uses his Twitter account to make announcements about new policies, changes within his administration, and according to Sean Spicer (former Press Secretary), President Trump's tweets are official statements. The court continued in their ruling by stating:

> *"...that the First Amendment does not permit a public official who utilizes a social media account for all manner of official purposes to exclude persons from an otherwise-open online dialogue because they expressed views with which the official disagrees."* – Judge Barrington D. Parker, July 9, 2019 via Case 18-1691, Document 141-1

This is exactly right. The public has a right to petition the government to redress grievances, and because President Trump had used his Twitter account in an official capacity he had opened up his account as a public forum where people should be free to both view his official comments, and redress their grievances by posting replies.

If in the Court of Appeals opinion, President Trump's Twitter account is now an official public forum protected under the laws of the United States; then meddling with President Trump's Twitter account is now tantamount to depriving the public of their first amendment rights. At the very least it's interfering with that process, and that's exactly what Twitter did. In May of 2020, in the middle of a global 'pandemic' Twitter sought to interfere with the first amendment rights of every United States citizen when they began labeling President Trump's tweets with fact checks. On May 26, 2020, President Trump tweeted the following statement in two separate tweets:

> *"There is NO WAY (ZERO!) that Mail-In Ballots will be anything less than substantially fraudulent. Mail boxes will be robbed, ballots will be forged & even illegally printed out & fraudulently signed. The Governor of California is sending Ballots to millions of people, anyone living in the state, no matter who they are or how they got there, will get one. That will be followed up with professionals telling all of these people, many of whom have never even thought of voting before, how, and for whom, to vote. This will be a Rigged Election. No way!"* - @RealDonaldTrump, May 26, 2020

Directly below each tweet? A blue link, stating, *"Get the facts about mail-in ballots"*. If a person clicks on that link, they're taken to a new page with a big, bold headline that reads, *Trump makes unsubstantiated claim that mail-in ballots will lead to voter fraud.* Below that appears to be a blurb from a CNN article that reads:

> *"On Tuesday, President Trump made a series of claims about potential voter fraud after California Governor Gavin Newsom announced an effort to expand mail-in voting in California during the covid-19 pandemic. These claims are unsubstantiated, according to CNN,*

> *Washington Post and others. Experts say mail-*
> *in ballots are very rarely linked to voter fraud."*
> - Twitter, May 26, 2020

An official Twitter account goes on to say:

> *"We added a label to two @realDonaldTrump*
> *Tweets about California's vote-by-mail plans as*
> *part of our efforts to enforce our civic integrity*
> *policy. We believe those Tweets could confuse*
> *voters about what they need to do to receive a*
> *ballot and participate in the election process."* -
> Twitter, May 27, 2020

The only problem is this fact check is itself unsubstantiated. And Twitter's response is clearly an attempt to interfere in a public forum clearly established by the 2nd U.S. Circuit Court of Appeals. Aside from that, isn't it the job of journalists to editorialize. Twitter is just a platform, isn't it? More on that in a later chapter. In their statement Twitter claims President Trump's tweets could confuse a voter about receiving a ballot. Nowhere, in any of President Trump's statements does he mislead, misstate, or attempt to deceive any person about how to physically vote, where to vote, when to vote, participate in voting, receive a mail in ballot, or absentee ballot to vote. On the contrary, President Trump clearly states he is concerned about rampant voter fraud that mail in voting is very susceptible to, and warning citizens of this danger.

What there is clear evidence of is mail-in voter fraud. Voter fraud exists, it's well documented, and there have been criminal convictions for people engaging in these illegal activities. Furthermore, over 28 million ballots have gone missing in the last 4 election cycles from 2012 to 2018. While missing ballots doesn't necessarily indicate fraud, that's an average of 7 million ballots that don't get counted, and after serving 5 years in the U.S. Marine Corps, I'd like my vote to count.

But those 28 million missing ballots aren't the only concern. There are numerous, documented instances of mail in ballots, and other voting materials being tampered with or systemically discarded. In October 2016, a postal worker was caught throwing away ballot guides in Berkeley, California. The U.S. Postal Service Office of the Inspector General launched an investigation after 96 ballot guides were found in a recycling bin. Thankfully, a citizen identified as Mr. Scott Wheeler found the ballot guides and called the proper authorities. Ironically, this wasn't the first time he had experienced a problem as a voter dealing with the post office. Mr. Wheeler had been deactivated as a voter, when the U.S. Post Office claimed he no longer lived at his home. His county's voter registrar received notification from the post office Mr. Wheeler no longer lived at that address and was subsequently deactivated. The problem is: he still lived at that address. Ostensibly the post office was still delivering his mail, to his address, so why would they send this notification in error? Wheeler says of the incident:

> *"I think this is incompetence and laziness probably rather than a conspiracy."* - Scott Wheeler, October 20, 2016 via NBC

Mr. Wheeler is probably right. I'm not certain if that makes the situation better or worse. One thing I'm certain of is that I don't want my vote, or the votes of millions of Americans delivered by people that are lazy or incompetent.

Concerns about voter fraud and election interference go beyond postal workers who are lazy or incompetent. There are also legitimate concerns people will engage in illegal activities. In Delaware, during the 2016 presidential election cycle, a postal worker, in full uniform and broad daylight was caught on camera stealing a Trump 2016 campaign yard sign from a private citizen. While this crime isn't voter fraud, it is a warning to the American people that at least one U.S. Post Office employee is willing to commit a crime to support their politics. During Spring of 2020, a U.S. Postal worker from West Virginia was caught tampering with ballots. Thomas Cooper eventually pled guilty to mail and election fraud after admitting he changed the political affiliation on multiple voter ballots from Democrat to Republican. This is election fraud, on ballots, substantiating President's Trumps assertions.

Even though the U.S.P.S. is a popular topic during this discussion, it's not just post-office employees committing crimes to influence election outcomes. Election officials are also guilty. Melowese Richardson was convicted in 2013 on four counts of voter fraud after accepting a plea deal that saw four additional charges dropped. She is a former Hamilton County, Ohio poll worker, and was sentenced to five years in prison for her crimes. She was convicted of voting as her sister in 2008, 2011, and 2012. What makes this even more despicable is that her sister has been in a coma since 2003. Was Richardson apologetic and remorseful? On the contrary she was combative, playing the victim, and claimed persecution at her sentencing stating:

> *"I think the board has shown me nothing but total disrespect for the 30 years I've served them. I believe in the system and I've done nothing to harm the system or cause disgrace to President Obama."* - Melowese Richardson, July 17, 2013

Judge Robert Ruehlman disagreed:

> *"This is not a little thing. It's not a minor thing. This is what our country's based on: free elections"* - Judge Robert Ruehlman, July 17, 2013

The prosecutor Bill Anderson agreed with Judge Ruehlman's assessment stating:

> *"her job is actually to protect the integrity and sanctity of the voting system. (She) is an ideologue who was hell bent on stuffing the ballot box with as many Obama votes as possible."* - Bill Anderson, July 17, 2013

Even Hamilton County Democratic Party Chair Tim Burke was disappointed by Richardson's behaviour stating:

> *"It's very sad how she doesn't understand how she abused the trust that was placed in her as a poll worker."* - Tim Burke, July 17, 2013 via The Cincinnati Enquirer

There were others from the battleground state of Ohio that were convicted of voter fraud. From a March 12, 2013 article published by the Huffington post and written by Dominique Mosbergen (Senior Reporter per their bio), 19 possible cases of voter fraud were under investigation. Per the article, Marguerite Kloos was indicted after she filled out an absentee ballot for another her friend, and fellow nun who died a month before the 2012 presidential election. Kloos also resigned from her role as Dean of the Division of Arts and Humanities at the College of Mount St. Joseph. There's also Russell Glassop, who submitted his wife's absentee ballot. The problem is she had died prior to casting her vote in 2012.

The list goes on, and the problems with mail in voting have been made even more abundantly clear in 2020, once again proving President Trump correct. In April 2020, there were thousands of absentee ballots across Wisconsin that went missing. In Fox Point, officials received 175 returned ballots from the U.S. Postal Service without explanation on the day of the election. Undelivered ballots from Appleton and Oshkosh were also found at a post office by a postal worker. Milwaukee Election Commission Executive Director Neil Albrecht claims that of all the absentee ballots issued, approximately 40,000 were not returned, or were missing. This meant the normal 90% return rate dropped to nearly 60%. Eventually around 23,000 absentee ballots were thrown out, or around 15% of voters that used absentee ballots didn't have their vote counted. In California, election officials discarded over 100,000 votes. In a state controlled by democrats, it's not shocking that such massive voter suppression occurred.

After all suppressing black, and republican votes is how they got their start.

Even though these discarded votes don't necessarily reflect fraud, they do reflect a profoundly serious problem our voting system clearly isn't prepared to handle. Counting a person's vote is equally as important as allowing them to vote. After all, what good is a vote if it gets thrown away. My question for Twitter, which I think should be every American's question is this: if all these incidents of voter fraud, and election tampering aren't substantiating evidence, what is? If we're to believe the line, "this election is too important" shouldn't we all be concerned about these types of incidents? If concerns about voting integrity are a genuine concern for Twitter, they should be highlighting these moments when we were actually able to catch the perpetrator. In a country where 1 in 3 murders go unsolved, which is the crime society is most dedicated to solving, there are certainly more instances of voter fraud and election tampering that are never discovered. Maybe Twitter's fact check is just another case of TDS gone awry. Regardless, an analysis of Twitter's actions is something everyone should do so they can form an opinion. Hopefully, the evidence and analysis provided above can help someone develop a more informed opinion.

Even if you're not on board with all the conservative conspiracy theories it cannot be denied that Twitter is willing to censor free speech and open communication when doing so serves its interests. In 2019, CPJ or the Committee to Protect Journalists (CPJ) released a report that claimed Twitter began undermining the free flow of information in Kashmir. After being pressured by the Indian government, Twitter actively deleted more than 1 million tweets, and began a systematic banning of accounts over the span of two years. These bans targeted citizens supporting civil disobedience as the Indian government sought to reign in political dissidents. The ban campaign Twitter led in Kashmir eventually represented bans and suspensions for more than all other countries combined. Impressive for a region with a population with around 5.5 million people. Worse yet, one of these bans was the Twitter account of a magazine that provided journalistic accounts of the unrest in the region. In a tweet dated October 25, 2019 Human Rights Watch Executive Director Kenneth Roth writes:

> *"The Indian government has been pressing Twitter to censor journalism and commentary emanating from Kashmir. Meanwhile, "more accounts were withheld in India in the second half of 2018 than in the rest of the world combined, according to Twitter." - @KenRoth October 25, 2019*

These actions are in stark contrast to sentiments given by a former Twitter Vice President Tony Wang. In March 2012, an article published at the Guardian, Tony claimed that Twitter is the:

> *"the free speech wing of the free speech party"* - Tony Wang, March 22, 2012

Apparently much had changed at Twitter in those 5 years. While this report only covers Twitter's behaviour in India and doesn't speak to their bias in American politics, it does make clear two things: Twitter is able to target specific groups of people sharing certain types of information, and they're willing to do so if it serves their needs.

Twitter's dominant position as a quick and portable communication tool is undeniable. The folks that oversee Twitter such as Jack Dorsey, one of the founders and current CEO know this, and he is, ostensibly, human. His politics are likely to guide his decision making, and as a private company (meaning non-state actor, yes, they are publicly traded) his role as CEO allows him to guide the company with his political bias. The Prager-U lawsuit has affirmed this.

Jack was asked about political bias by Sam Harris on his podcast, Making Sense. During the interview Sam discusses the disciplinary actions such as suspensions and bans for rule violations appear to, *"reliably land on one side of the political divide.*" Jack's response: *"I don't believe [Twitter] can afford to, take a neutral stance anymore."* At least he's honest. Jack goes on to attempt to hedge and explain his differentiation between neutrality and impartiality. While there is some nuance there, at this point just lean in and say, "Yes. Twitter is a platform that heavily favors liberal democrat ideology." Maybe Jack feels that type of clear statement would cause a stock dip. People might not be as excited to invest in a company that is an active disinformant. This would probably be true over a short run, however investors won't be easily dissuaded to divest from a profitable company or surrender a valuable marketing arena over a spat about politics. I do think these investors are not calculating the total costs. By allowing companies like Twitter to control such wide bands of information flow, society is slowing careening towards disaster.

chapter 5: okay, google

Most people don't know the company Alphabet Inc. In fact, if asked, someone might google them to find out. Ironically, they already knew the answer because they just took an action named after the company that has come to dominate the internet. Alphabet Inc is the parent company for Google, which was founded in 1998. After some restructuring in 2015, the iconic brand name became a subsidiary, but still holds sway over how most people know the company. With over $161 billion dollars in revenue, Fortune.com lists them (Alphabet Inc / Google) as the 29th largest company in the world. More than 90% of all search traffic on the internet is managed by Google. How does Google wield their apparent monopolistic power and place as trusted authority for information? By manipulating search results to favor the Democratic Party.

Despite Mr. Pichai's congressional testimony, Google does in fact manipulate the search results they provide. In fact, an article published on CNBC.com states:

"Google knowingly manipulates search results according to a research paper published Monday from several academics." - Mark Bergen, June 29, 2015 via CNBC

The academic paper the article cites was written by a Tim Wu who is described as a legal scholar, and former FTC advisor. In the paper, the author's describe Google as intentionally denying the best search results to their users.

"the easy and widely disseminated argument that Google's universal search always serves users and merchants is demonstrably false." - Tim Wu, June 29, 2015

While these findings were limited to the scope of commerce rather than political searches, it is a testimony that Google has the technological capability to intentionally manipulate search results, they are willing to intentionally manipulate search results, and they lack the ethical boundaries to prevent them from engaging in this type of behaviour.

In 2016 an individual named Dr. Robert Epstein (of no relation to the notorious convicted pedophile and child rapist Jeffrey Epstein who did not kill himself) conducted a study where he claims up to 10.4 million voters may have been directly influenced due to a bias in Google search results. In an interview by Mark Levin, Dr. Epstein claims in his study he:

> *"...looked at politically oriented searches that these people were conducting on Google, Bing and Yahoo. I was able to preserve more than 13,000 searches and 98,000 web pages, and I found very dramatic bias in Google's search results favoring Hillary Clinton, whom I supported strongly."* - Dr. Epstein, September 8, 2019

Dr. Epstein continues by explaining:

> *"...if a search result that's high up on the list, if that takes you to a web page that makes one candidate look better than another, if you're undecided and you're trying to make up your mind, what we've learned is that information posted high in Google search results will shift opinions among undecided people dramatically because people trust Google."* - Dr. Epstein, September 8, 2019

Critics of the study rightly point out that while there were 95 participants in the study, only around 20 were undecided voters, and the sample size is too small to accurately extrapolate across a diverse nation, with a large population, and a group of voters that sits around 138 million. While these criticisms are accurate and Dr. Epstein's study doesn't outright prove Google actively engages in politically motivated social engineering, it is evidentiary of political bias at Google.

Steering a conversation is like boiling frogs. Turn too abruptly and people will see through the turn. Slowly guide the conversation, and they may not notice for hours. Even though this fable was disproven for frogs, scientists have identified a similar behaviour in humans and have termed it creeping normality. This is when large or fundamental change might be rejected, so smaller, incremental changes towards the larger change are taken without people noticing much. This might be closer to the strategy Google has taken, because during the 2016 election cycle, they appeared to make subtle changes to autofill search recommendations, removing negative search suggestions that might have produced articles that hurt the chances for then presidential candidate Hillary Clinton.

In a report by the now shuttered Sourcefed, journalist and editor Spencer Reed identified a small quirk in his autofill box when it came to performing searching for the various presidential candidates. At the time there were several hot button issues nagging the candidates, and for Hillary one of those was the fact she used a private email server to conduct official government business during her time as Secretary of State. The trouble is that her use of a private email server for communicating classified materials is at the very least willfully negligent, if not in direct violation of federal law.

The full extent of her crime will never be known as her team also deleted around 30,000 emails effectively destroying evidence. Regardless of Hillary's misdeeds and how they impacted U.S. foreign policy, the email issue was a thorn in the side for her 2016 campaign, and a point of interest for potential voters that year. According to the report by Sourcefed, this email issue, and other issues that might have been viewed as hurtful to a Hillary election were not auto filling into Google's search recommendations. The report stated that a simple search compared the phrase, "Hillary Clinton cri" on Google, versus other search engines. On Google, this search would return autofill recommendations such as "Hillary Clinton crime reform".

What did two other search engines autofill features recommend? Bing and Yahoo auto filled with "Hillary Clinton criminal investigation" and "Hillary Clinton crime". Sourcefed admitted in their report that this could be explained away by differences in the competitors search algorithms, however upon closer review of Google's trend tool, the search for "Hillary Clinton crime reform" didn't pull enough results to form a trend. This would indicate that such a search was not commonly searched as Google uses information searches performed by all users when making suggestions in their autofill results. This also aligns with Dr. Epstein's study that claimed Google was altering search results.

Google's excuse? In response posted by Tamar Yehoshua, Director of Product Management, on June 10, 2016, they state:

"The autocomplete algorithm is designed to avoid completing a search for a person's name with terms that are offensive or disparaging."

Tamar goes on to say:

"Predictions are produced based on a number of factors including the popularity and freshness of search terms."

Again, I would point out that the Sourcefed report indicated that the phrase, "Hillary Clinton crime reform" had not returned enough searches to form a trend, so how could it be the leading recommendation?

While these stories are not a smoking gun for Google directly interfering during the 2016 election there are times when Google has been explicitly caught pushing the leftist agenda. In 2017 when President Trump proposed a travel ban for certain countries that actively support terrorist activities, a group of Google employees were documented in an email chain openly discussing ways to manipulate search results. This was confirmed by Google itself in a statement they released:

"These emails were just a brainstorm of ideas, none of which were ever implemented. Google has never manipulated its search results or modified any of its products to promote a particular political ideology. Not in the current campaign season, not during the 2016 election, and not in the aftermath of President Trump's executive order on immigration. Our processes and policies would not have allowed for any manipulation of search results to promote political ideologies." - Google, September 20, 2018

That's kind of like the wolf saying they were just looking at the sheep, they would never attack one. What's odd about that statement is the juxtaposition it compared to a leaked video obtained by Breitbart a few days earlier. In the video that was recorded days after the 2016 election, it's clear that the top leaders at Google are interested in what Google can do to prevent it from happening again. The video is about an hour-long diatribe about how awful President Trump is. At around a minute into the video, Google founder Sergey Brin says:

"I certainly find this election deeply offensive, and I know many of you do too."

Brin goes on to say the election:

"conflicts with many of our values."

Google's values conflict with the democratic election of a U.S. president? That statement alone says more about Google than it does about anything else. It wasn't just Sergey Brin that seemed to have an issue with American voters. In the same video around 5 minutes in, Ruth Porat, Google's CFO said Google will:

> *"use the great strength and resources and*
> *reach we have to continue to advance really*
> *important values."*

So, we have several Google executives explicitly stating Google will use its power to influence voters to align with their values. Values that apparently conflict with a democratic election.

The video features several speakers, and questions asked by Google employees in the audience. One moment that stands out is when Sergey Brin speaks at around 34 minutes into the video. Here Brin presents his analysis of the data surrounding voters commenting on Hillary winning voters making under $100,000. He goes on observing in his mind that Trump voters had jobs which were as he describes, *"routine"*. Routine jobs are often described as middle-class jobs. Rather than observing that President Trump had connected with, and continues to defend the middle class American, Brin derides them by calling their votes a case of boredom, and then correlates that to extremism, and later in the video, blames it for the rise of fascism. Brin goes further by saying that, *"voting is not a rational act"*.

Again, this video, and Dr. Epstein's study, are not 'gotcha' moments. They're evidence to demonstrate that Google employees are actively engaged in subverting conservative viewpoints and conservative voices. In an email sent by Eliana Murillo shortly after the 2016 election demonstrates this bias. The email written by a department head at Google was titled, *Election results and the Latino vote* as quoted by Breitbart. Murillo claimed she was a part of a team of Google employees that made efforts to pay for free rides as a part of a get-out-the-vote program targeted at Hispanic voters. Murillo felt that this would be a non-partisan activity, which they used to mask their effort to help elect Hillary during the 2016 election. In her email, as quoted by Breitbart, she states:

> *"We also supported partners like Voto Latino to*
> *pay for rides to the polls in key states (silent*

donation). We even helped them create ad campaigns to promote the rides (with support from HOLA folks who rallied and volunteered their time to help). We supported Voto Latino to help them land an interview with Senator Meza of Arizona (key state for us) to talk about the election and how to use Google search to find information about how to vote. They were a strong partner, among many in this effort." - Eliana Murillo, November 9, 2016

It should be noted that Voto Latino is led by democratic operative, Maria Teresa Kumar and is considered a left leaning organization. However, Murillo's most damning testimony regarding Google's apparent political bias is this:

"Ultimately, after all was said and done, the Latino community did come out to vote, and completely surprised us. We never anticipated that 29% of Latinos would vote for Trump. No one did. We saw headlines like this about early voter turnout and thought that this was finally the year that the 'sleeping giant' had awoken." - Eliana Murillo, November 9, 2016

Murillo continues later in her email with this:

"This is devastating for our Democratic Latino community. After all these efforts and what we thought was positive momentum toward change, the results are not what we expected at all. We are afraid for our families, and especially for the millions of immigrants who now don't know what the future holds for them." - Eliana Murillo, November 9, 2016

If Murillo, and by proxy, Google, were genuinely interested in supporting non-partisan activities by engaging voters, why should it be surprising that the Latino community would vote for President Trump? Why is it devastating that 29% of Latino voters chose President Trump as the candidate that best represented their communities? Why would she term the Latino community the *"sleeping giant"* that needed to be woken up? If the intention of Murillo and her team were truly non-partisan, wouldn't her efforts be positive in getting more Latinos engaged in voting? Regardless of who they voted for, shouldn't Murillo and her team be excited they accomplished their mission? Unless their mission was to elect Hillary Clinton, meaning their motivations were in fact, extremely partisan. I'm not alone in that observation, Google's own Product Marketing Manager MacKenzie Thomas wrote in a separate email:

> *"Forwarding this not because of the original sender but rather how explicitly it references that her work was 100% partisan."* -
> Mackenzie Thomas, November 2016

If this isn't direct and explicit evidence of the political bias promulgated at Google, I'm not sure what would be. How about an 85-page document also leaked to Breitbart titled, *The Good Censor How can Google reassure the world that it protects users from harmful content while still supporting free speech?* from March of 2018. I'm not certain they could have written that question in a more patronizing manner. Google is not my daddy. I don't need, or want Google protecting me from what they deem harmful. Not only is Google's presumption to take such a role offensive, it is the very definition of fascism.

Written by and disseminated to Google employees, the good censor is an 85-page document that outlines why Google should use their power to censor the internet. To protect us, of course. It opens with a statement where Google claims:

> *"...debates about who can and should be heard on the internet rage like never before."* -
> Google, March 2018

The only people debating about who can and should be on the internet are the liberal gestapo seeking to silence wrongthink. It's a farce to believe anyone but liberals want to censor voices from the internet. It's an opt in community, if a person doesn't want to hear or read something, they are literally one click from blocking, filtering, or navigating away. Google confirms this when the note that:

> *"Unhappy with the level of censorship on certain platforms, users are emigrating to ones with more, or less, restrictive rules."* - Google, March 2018

Google continues by stating:

> *"...Twitter tries to counteract this by taking on a more curatorial and moderatorial role, communities that disagree with these changes are moving to less restrictive platforms."* - Google, March 2018

These two statements directly undercut Google's argument that there's a need for a 'good censor'. Google also claims:

> *"...users are asking if the openness of the internet should be celebrated after all."* - Google, March 2018

Again, the only people asking if the openness of the internet are liberal fascists attempting to silence wrongthink. The rise of the internet is directly tied to the very ideal of freedom. Google knows this because they quote John Barlow's declaration of independence of cyberspace. In it he says:

> *"Governments of the Industrial World, you weary giants of flesh and steel, I come from Cyberspace, the new home of Mind. On behalf*

of the future, I ask you of the past to leave us alone. You are not welcome among us. You have no sovereignty where we gather." - John Barlow, February 8, 1996

In fact, all tech companies know this. Google's own founders Larry Page and Sergey Brin stated in 2004 in their IPO letter:

"We have also emphasized an atmosphere of creativity and challenge, which has helped us provide unbiased, accurate and free access to information for those who rely on us around the world." - Sergey Brin & Larry Page, 2004

The very existence of this 'good censor' document is anathema to that statement. It seems 16 years of rising power and authority have had a corrupting influence, or as my friend puts it, a magnifying effect on Sergey.

Google also claims that, *"Free speech becomes a social, economic and political weapon"* and here they are actually correct. That's because free speech has always been a weapon, and it will always be a weapon against those that seek to control others. Free speech was a weapon used by our greatest leaders to drive the civil rights movement. Martin Luther King Jr. inspired millions and inspired an entire generation of social change. He used freedom of speech, a right protected by an imperfect society, in his efforts to drive positive change. He did not use force to impose his will on others. He used the power of speech. Surely, he was willing to use force in the defense of his life but knew the absolute power that free thought holds. He used that power in his efforts to tear down injustice. When Adam Smith wrote Wealth of Nations, this single exercise in free speech provided the very foundation of economic change lifting billions of people, across generations, and in every nation, out of poverty. And free speech is the last weapon being used in Hong Kong by protesters seeking respite from the tyrannical Chinese Communist Party. With free speech Hong Kong residents seeking the freedom they were promised write messages of hope, messages seeking support, and messages warning the world that humanity must never surrender to communist tyranny. This is the free speech Google seeks to control and undermine as the 'good censor'.

Google continues as it argues tech companies are, *"performing a balancing act between two incompatible positions…".* Those positions? On one side they list: American traditions - a marketplace of ideas, a commitment to free speech, democracy, and open debate. The other side: European traditions - dignity over liberty, and civility over freedom, and censorship. Which side has Google chosen? They openly admit a gradual shift towards censorship where they are politicized publishers. In fact, they indict Facebook and Twitter as well as participating in these shifts.

When Google asks, *"who should be responsible for censoring 'unwanted' conversation, anyway?"* The resounding answer: nobody. Each individual is responsible for censoring unwanted conversations in a digital world where they are one click away from the next page. Barlow made it clear governments weren't welcome, and as more people become aware of Google's insidious nature, more and more users are realizing Google should not be the one to make those decisions either, and when they engage in the behaviours described in this chapter, they are in fact behaving as a disinformant.

chapter 6: in your facebook

Facebook is the app we all hate to love. We can connect with loved ones and far away friends, we can share our lives with the people around us, but mostly we argue with people we rarely see, about things we know very little about, in an effort to get more likes and attention. Facebook was founded in 2004 by Mark Zuckerberg and a few of his Harvard roommates. By 2012 Facebook was prepared to go public, and their IPO raised $16 billion dollars. It was the third largest U.S. IPO at the time. Eight years later in 2020 Facebook reported around 2.7 billion monthly active users making it the largest social media company. With a market that large, Facebook was able to generate around $70 billion dollars in revenue in 2019 and has used their success to purchase several other technology companies including Instagram, WhatsApp, and Oculus VR.

What else has Facebook been doing with that success? Flashback to the 2016 election cycle. President Trump uttered the phrase, 'fake news' and it began to gain traction. Due in part to the building frustration people felt towards corporate media outlets, and their deceptive reporting practices. However, the idea of fake news was a subject that had been a rising concern for some years, particularly at Facebook. So much so, that in June of 2015, the same month President Trump officially announced his candidacy for president, an organization called First Draft was formed. First Draft's mission is, *"to protect communities from harmful misinformation"*. They were founded by several groups and charitable donors, including Google, Twitter, and guess who, Facebook. Don't worry though, just like Google has, *"don't be evil,"* Twitter is, *"committed to protecting freedom of speech"*, and Facebook isn't an, *"arbiter of truth"*, First Draft is also definitely not biased. Their statement of independence clearly states:

> *"First Draft is a non-partisan organization. It has no political affiliation, and does not accept*

funding from governments or political parties" -
First Draft

First Draft categorizes fake news into several categories
including the following:

1. ***Fabricated content:*** *information that is
   completely false with the intent to deceive.*

2. ***False context:*** *when accurate information
   is presented without the circumstances
   necessary to understand the meaning of the
   information presented.*

3. ***False connection:*** *when the content of
   presented material isn't connected to the
   headline.*

4. ***Manipulated content:*** *this is when
   accurate information is presented in a
   deceptive manner.*

5. ***Misleading content:*** *using information to
   present a topic in a particular light.*

6. ***Impostor content:*** *when a trusted source
   is impersonated as to add veracity to
   information.*

7. ***Satire:*** *the use of parody, humor, or
   exaggeration when discussing a particular
   topic.*

Number 7 on that list is interesting because satire, and
parody stories usually announce themselves and aren't
generally considered harmful fake news but rather obvious
comedic attempts at political commentary. If First Draft's
mission is to protect communities from harmful
information, why would fake news include satire? For

example, the Onion is a well-known parody site and they have headlines such as, *Cat-Eared, Pink-Haired Bill Clinton Exhorts DNC Viewers To Donate For Access To Uncensored Version Of Speech.* Clearly over the top satire and most people reading anything linked to the Onion are aware the stories there are satire.

However, newcomers to the satire scene may not enjoy that same ubiquity. The Babylon Bee for example is newer than the Onion and puts a conservative lens on satire. To combat the confusion and prevent someone from mistaking their satire for fake news, they clearly announce themself a satirical website. The Bee was founded in 2016 by a man named Adam Ford who gave this statement when he sold it:

> *"Facebook has the power to kill publishers, and they do, not only based on publishing techniques, but based on worldview. Just think about that."* – Adam Ford via adam4d.com

Why would a successful content creator who just sold a popular website be so jaded about Facebook? Maybe because despite their self-declared boast that they are, *"...the world's best satire site, totally inerrant in all its truth claims"*, Facebook's fact check team has launched attacks against them several times for clearly satirical articles.

On March 1st, 2018 the Babylon Bee published an article titled, *CNN Purchases Industrial-Sized Washing Machine To Spin News Before Publication,* which is clearly satire. At the time a Snopes.com was a part of that Facebook fact check team and flagged the article as false. No problem, they probably just flagged it satire and now people will know. Only that's not the story, because until late 2019, Snopes didn't have a satire rating. What Facebook did was issue a threat to page administrator Adam Ford. In it they write:

> *"A page you admin (The Babylon Bee) recently posted the link (CNN Purchases Industrial-Sized Washing Machine to Spin News Before*

Publication) that contains info disputed by (Snopes.com), an independent fact checker. Repeat offenders will see their distribution reduced and their ability to monetize and advertise removed."

Eventually Facebook backed down, and in a statement to The Daily Caller News foundation said:

"There's a difference between false news and satire. This was a mistake and should not have been rated false in our system. It's since been corrected and won't count against the domain in any way."

Clearly Facebook realized their error, issued an apology, and moving forward will recognize that satire should not be flagged fake news. Wrong again. Snopes instead chose to escalate their campaign of harassment against the conservative satirical website. Over the next year Snopes continued to issue fact check labels to articles the Babylon Bee published marking them fake news. On July 22, 2019 the Babylon Bee published an article titled, *Georgia Lawmaker Claims Chick-Fil-A Employee Told Her To Go Back To Her Country, Later Clarifies He Actually Said 'My Pleasure'*, as satirical commentary on a contemporary political subject. Remember the Babylon Bee is self-described as the, *"...world's best satire..."* and Facebook has declared that there is in fact a difference between false news and satire. So why the fact checks by Snopes? If Snopes applied their journalistic standard in the same fashion as to other satire sites such as the Onion, it would dispel any notion that there was a political bias at work. However, the Babylon Bee is satire with a conservative slant, poking fun at democratic politicians and liberal stereotypes. Though this discussion may be moot at this point as Snopes and Facebook had parted ways in early of 2019 it does lend credence to the political bias within Facebook for enabling an organization such as Snopes, going as far as making them a key member of their fact check team. Again, this is not direct evidence that Facebook intentionally targets and suppresses conservative voices. It is circumstantial evidence, and a preponderance of circumstantial evidence would be sufficient to make that assertion reasonable.

Snopes wasn't the only company Facebook partnered with to combat fake news. PolitiFact was and remains another organization Facebook partners with for fact checking articles. Founded in 2007 as a project by the Poynter Institute they created the 'truth-o-meter' rating. Don't worry they're completely unbiased. How do we know? Because just like Google, Twitter, and Facebook, they say so. A person navigating their page can find a section under the About Us heading titled, *Our Process*. On this page PolitiFact claims:

> *"Our core principles are independence, transparency, fairness, thorough reporting and clear writing. The reason we publish is to give citizens the information they need to govern themselves in a democracy"* - PolitiFact

A laudable goal. However, the fact check labels they apply appear to directly contradict Facebook's alleged neutrality. During 2020 several cities, primarily run by democrats, saw violent riots sweep across their neighborhoods. These riots were led by people chanting things like, *"death to America"*, claiming that they had a right to loot, and promoting slogans such as, *"all cops are bastards"*. Government officials even gave their tacit approval for these destructive behaviours that include the shooting of law enforcement personnel, arson, and looting of small businesses. In September of 2020, Lynwood City Manager Jose Ometeotl posted an image on his Instagram account showing Malcom X and the caption, "CHICKENS COME HOME TO ROOST" in response to two LA county sheriff's being shot in a violent ambush. In another instance Contra Costa County District Attorney Diane Becton outlined guidelines that their office would prosecute looters under. Included in

Becton's instructions prosecutors were directed to consider the *"needs"* of the suspected looter.

This dereliction of sworn duties by liberal democratic politicians left citizens with little recourse. Much like the 1992 LA riots the failure of the local government forced responsible citizens, acting for the good of their communities and neighbors, to step into action and deter the wide scale destruction. It became particularly poignant during the nationwide 2020 riots because the violent and destructive behaviour was seemingly encouraged by democratic mayors and city councils calling to defund police departments. One such citizen who was forced to defend his neighbors was 17-year-old Kyle Rittenhouse. In raw video footage captured by multiple sources, Kyle is seen extinguishing a dumpster fire near a gas station that was set by terrorists. In subsequent videos Mr. Rittenhouse is seen fleeing for his life, being chased by multiple attackers. One of the attackers threw what appears to be a brick at Mr. Rittenhouse who then defended his life. In a separate video a person is seen jumping on and kicking Mr. Rittenhouse, which is followed immediately by another person assaulting him with a skateboard and again Mr. Rittenhouse is forced to defend his life. While still on the ground Mr. Rittenhouse is attacked once more by a man wielding a handgun and again, Mr. Rittenhouse is forced to defend himself. All this information is readily available in unedited, raw footage form. As of this writing, Mr. Rittenhouse has been charged with several crimes, and on August 31, 2020 President Trump stated in a press conference:

> *"That was an interesting situation. You saw the same tape as I saw. He was trying to get away from them, I guess, looks like. And he fell and then they very violently attacked him. And it was something that we're looking at right now, and it's under investigation, but I guess he was in very big trouble. He probably would have been killed. It's under investigation."*

All of those are factually correct statements except for maybe his assertion that they saw the same tape.

1. Is this topic interesting, check, or presumably the press wouldn't be asking President Trump for comment.

2. [Kyle] was trying to get away from [attackers], check, confirmed in multiple videos.

3. [Kyle] fell, check, confirmed in multiple videos.

4. Violently attacked, I would argue being attacked with a brick and a skateboard is a violent attack, check, confirmed in multiple videos.

5. Something [president] is looking at, check, self-admitted.

6. Under investigation, check, confirmed by both the news media asking the question to President Trump, and via the pending legal prosecution.

7. [Kyle] was in very big trouble, seems like an opinion but I would again argue being chased by multiple attackers as big trouble, check, confirmed in multiple videos.

8. [Kyle] probably would have been killed, being that one of [Kyle's] attackers threw a brick at him, and a second attacker had a handgun, check, confirmed in multiple videos.

A slam dunk for anyone going to fact check President Trump this time. True or Mostly True. Except that's not what PolitiFact claims. The 'fact check' published by PolitiFact rates President Trump's statement "False", their second lowest rating. The article states:

> *"But Trump's claim leaves out vital context: that Rittenhouse ran away from protesters after prosecutors say he had already shot and killed someone"* - Haley BeMiller, August 31, 2020

This is 'half true' to use a term the writer might understand. Prosecutors have **alleged** Haley's version of events happened. This timeline of events hasn't been proven and is thus, not a fact. Not only has this version of events not been proven, all evidence available at the time of this writing demonstrates this narrative is false. As a journalist it is reckless to present a prosecutor's allegations as a fact and doing so may constitute defamation.

Haley continues her argument when she writes, *"it's unclear what, if any, investigation would still be open"*. A murder investigation. That's literally how our legal system works. In a post by National Crime Victim Law Institute, they state:

> *"...discovery is the pretrial process by which the prosecutor and the defendant exchange information and material about the case. Discovery is an intricate process governed by each jurisdiction's rules of criminal procedure"* - National Crime Victim Law Institute, April 15, 2010

Investigations don't end when charges are brought against a defendant and it seems like an exchange of information is literally what takes place during an investigation. However, if Haley is separating discovery from investigation, then perhaps guidance provided by the American Bar Association will provide some insight. The American Bar

Association literally sets academic standards for law schools, and writes the ethical codes followed by legal professionals. While not a formal state actor, the ABA is the authoritative body for practicing attorneys, and they give specific guidelines for prosecutors. Specifically, from their website:

> *"Standard 3-4.2 Decisions to Charge Are the Prosecutor's section (c): In determining whether formal criminal charges should be filed, prosecutors should consider whether further investigation should be undertaken. After charges are filed the prosecutor should oversee law enforcement investigative activity related to the case."* - American Bar Association, 2017

I'm not a professional, paid reporter, investigating the veracity of statements made by political or government officials, but with 30 minutes of effort I was able to perform a fact check about criminal investigations. Regardless, as of this writing, PolitiFact still asserts President Trump's statement is false.

PolitiFact appears complicit in the political bias of their contributor, and acting as a proxy for Facebook, presents President Trump in a negative light. PolitiFact wasn't the only 'trusted' news source pushing this narrative. NPR jumped into the fray with this tweet:

> *"President Trump declined to condemn the actions of the 17-year-old accused of shooting 3 protesters, killing 2, in Kenosha. Instead, he defended him. Claiming, without evidence, that it appeared the gunman was acting in self-defense."* - @nprpolitics, September 1, 2020

President Trump did decline to condemn Mr. Rittenhouse, because there is substantial video evidence that Mr. Rittenhouse acted in self-defense. Another way to phrase this would have been:

> *"President Trump declined to condemn the
> actions of the 17-year-old accused of shooting 3
> protesters, killing 2, in Kenosha. Instead, he
> defended him. Trump cited online videos as
> evidence the gunman was acting in self-
> defense."*

This potential headline would remain accurate, without appearing to take a political stance, the job of a journalist. When journalists engage in this type of biased reporting it constitutes a clear attempt to control information and reshape opinions of the public. These types of fact checks and headlines move the conversation from fringe conspiracy theory, to demonstrable fact that there is a concerted effort to push a liberal democrat narrative, and it's this type of manipulated content presented as a fact check that exemplifies TDS at its finest. It is especially frustrating knowing that Facebook instituted fact checks to combat fake news, and an entire category of fake news is titled manipulated content.

Facebook is taking it a step further with Kyle Rittenhouse. In their attempts to silence public opinion they have begun banning people for posting images in support of Kyle. Facebook claims it is based on their community standards stating:

> *"We don't allow symbols, praise, or support of
> dangerous individuals or organizations on
> Facebook. We define dangerous as things like:
> terrorist activity, organized hate or violence,
> mass or serial murder, human trafficking,
> criminal or harmful activity"*

This categorization by Facebook may constitute an assertion of guilt and venture into defamation territory because Kyle Rittenhouse has not been convicted of any crime to date. Additionally Facebook has taken the stance that Kyle is a dangerous individual despite the clear video evidence that shows he was forced to defend his life against numerous deadly attacks, Facebook is simultaneously allowing #freeChrystulKizer posts, and groups in support of Chrystul Kizer who is currently accused of murder.

While I don't know all the facts of the case, it appears the Chrystul Kizer case was also an act of self-defense after facing years of abuse by an accused pedophile. Still, the difference in application of standards is where Facebook runs afoul of those that cry political bias. Still not convinced? As of September 7, 2020, there are also multiple posts, groups, and organized events in support of Jacob Blake, who was shot 7 times by police. Jacob Blake was actively engaged in criminal activity when he was shot by police officers. Beyond that, Mr. Blake also has numerous pending violent criminal charges. While these alleged crimes may not warrant any person being shot 7 times, the fact remains that Jacob Blake is no less dangerous a person than Kyle Rittenhouse. Per Facebook's own standards, posts in support of him should not be allowed. However, banning people and posts in support of Chrystul, Darius, or Jacob Blake doesn't fit the narrative being driven by Facebook. They seem intent on only banning posts about Kyle Rittenhouse because this aligns with the liberal narratives being pushed by disinformants.

Things only get worse from there. Facebook also allowed the active organization of at least one event featuring a known, and documented terrorist. Promoted by SFSU students, the event titled, *Whose Narrative? Gender, Justice, & Resistance: A conversation with Leila Khaled,* was as of this writing, scheduled for September 23, 2020. For anyone wondering who Leila Khaled is, she is an active member of Popular Front for the Liberation of Palestine (PFLP). The PFLP is a terrorist organization that espouses marxist ideals. They have committed numerous terrorist attacks including plane hijackings, bombings, and mass executions. Famously Leila was a part of the TWA flight 840 hijacking, and the Dawson's Field hijackings. These two hijackings were notable for several reasons. One of those reasons being that airplane hijackings were a relatively new method used by terrorist organizations such as the PFLP. The second reason: female terrorists are unusual, and Khaled was the first female to hijack an airplane.

TWA flight 840 was hijacked on August 29, 1969 by Khaled and her accomplice. The flight was redirected to Syria which the terrorists referred to as a 'friendly country'. Throughout the hijacking Khaled and her accomplice would terrorize the passengers by threatening to blow up the airplane when it landed. Eventually the plane landed and the passengers in fear for their lives were able to evacuate the airplane. The joy was short lived however as many of the passengers were Jewish, and they were now in Syria, a country that had been humiliated by Israel during the Six Day War just two years earlier. The passengers were rounded up by Syrian forces and taken to different locations to be interrogated. Eventually Italy was able to negotiate for the release of the passengers, and Syria relented allowing all but two Israeli hostages free. The two remaining were traded for a Syrian pilot being held in prison. The hijacking had been a success for the PFLP and Khaled who was released back to Jordan.

A little more than a year later Khaled would again take part in terrorist activities. This time in a bold PFLP plot to hijack several airplanes at once. The Dawson's Field hijackings as they are now known took place in September 1970. Three out of four of the hijacked airplanes were redirected to an airstrip called Dawson's Field in Jordan. Khaled was the terrorist aboard the fourth airplane. El Al flight 219 was a flight originally bound to New York from Tel Aviv. Khaled was able to board the flight using a fake passport and posing as a married tourist. Once the plane was airborne, Khaled and her fellow terrorist used guns and grenades in their attempt to seize control of the airplane. During an interview with Philip Baum, Khaled states:

> *"...I rushed, reached to the cockpit, it was closed. So I was screaming open the door. Then the hostess came, she said "[Khaled] has two hand grenades", but they did not open (the cockpit door) and suddenly I was threatening to blow up the plane. I was saying I will count and if you don't open I will blow up the plane"* -
Leila Khaled, September 2000

During the struggle for control of the airplane, the terrorists shot a passenger who and later recovered. Khaled's accomplice was also shot, and he died of his wounds. Having subdued their attackers, the crew was able to make an emergency landing at Heathrow airport in London where Khaled was arrested. A little less than a month later Khaled was once again released, this time in exchange for British hostages.

Do not be fooled by the dates of her terrorist plots. These are not the wanton acts of a misguided youth. Khaled is a violent criminal that encourages others to participate in violence. In a 2016 interview with Leila Ettachfini, associate editor at Vice, Khaled states:

> *"I was happy because I was doing something for my people"* - Leila Khaled, June 2016 via Vice

She was happy to be participating in terrorist activities. Not misguided, or misled. Happy. Ettachfini writes of the flight 840 incident:

> *"...Khaled knows that her actions did, of course, frighten the innocent passengers, but to [Khaled], their momentary fear was a small price to pay..."* - Leila Ettachfini, August 4, 2016 via Vice

In another interview given in 2016 with Euronews, Khaled states:

> *"Some use words, some use arms and some use politics. Some use negotiations. I chose arms and I believe that taking up arms is one of the main tools to solve this (Palestinian-Israeli) conflict..."* - Leila Khaled, June 30, 2016 via Euronews

In the same article Khaled continues her violent rhetoric and says:

> *"this is a historical conflict. It cannot be solved by negotiations…"* - Leila Khaled, June 30, 2016 via Euronews

SFSU is correct in their assertion that Khaled speaking is protected by our first amendment, and they should be lauded for defending this fundamental right. Individual liberty means having the right to say disagreeable things, and to read or hear disagreeable things. This right should be of paramount importance in a society where freedom of speech is the very first right codified. In their defense of this freedom, the university provided the following statement:

> *"An invitation to a public figure to speak to a class should not be construed as an endorsement of point of view. Higher education and the college experience are an opportunity to hear divergent ideas, viewpoints and accounts of life experiences."* - SFSU, September 2020

I would take that a step further and say that any ***society*** that places value in individual liberty has an obligation to allow divergent ideas and viewpoints and accounts of life experiences to be shared. But that includes all viewpoints. Even when those ideas may be disagreeable to some people, which includes voicing support for Kyle Rittenhouse, or Jacob Blake.

I know extremely little about SFSU outside of this specific incident, and while they are a state funded institute and have a responsibility to allow a variety of viewpoints equally, Facebook has no such responsibility. As CEO, Mark Zuckerberg is free to run Facebook as far as the shareholders and board of directors will allow him. If that means Facebook doesn't defend free speech or create an egalitarian space for all voices that is their choice as a business. In that case let's dispel the notion that Facebook is such a place. That means despite what the company might claim Facebook has become the arbiters of what truths people can see, think, and say. Facebook is an active disinformant.

Instituting politically biased fact checking, and censoring unflattering facts aren't the only way Facebook seeks to control the flow of information. Facebook also actively suppressed conservative news. An article published by Gizmodo in 2016 claims that:

> *"Facebook workers routinely suppressed news stories of interest to conservative readers from the social network's influential "trending" news section..."* - Michael Nunez, May 9, 2016 via Gizmodo

Gizmodo's source told them stories about conservative politicians, and conservative topics were directly suppressed from appearing in this news section even if those topics were trending naturally. A second Gizmodo source agreed, and stated:

> *"it was absolutely biased. We were doing it subjectively. It just depends on who the curator is and what time of day it is. Every once in a while a Red State or conservative news source would have a story. But we would have to go and find the same story from a more neutral outlet that wasn't as biased"* - anonymous source, May 9, 2016 via Gizmodo

Worse still, the Gizmodo sources revealed that they were instructed to insert certain stories, presumably so Facebook could push a particular narrative. This type of editorialization is common among publishers. Just not the actions of a non-editorial platform, and certainly not the actions of a company that claims they are not *"arbiters of the truth."*

Going beyond goaltending conservative thoughts, voices, and views, Facebook is also actively protecting democratic politicians. On August 11, 2020, the democratic nominee for president, which is shockingly Joe Biden, allegedly selected Kamala Harris as his running mate. She was a great pick for the politician that helped institute racism in the U.S. judicial system as she had also built a career on incarcerating low-income minorities. Don't believe me? Check out kamalaharris.info. There are 6 topics covering her policy positions, demonstrating these facts with the sources linked as well. It would be nice to share this with my Facebook friends so they could make a more informed decision about who to vote for.

The only issue was, I couldn't post it to my timeline. Facebook was actively blocking any post containing this link. A link to a website that contained factually accurate, and in context reporting from the Daily Beast, the New York Times, Huffington Post, FactCheck.org, and others. Why would Facebook prevent legitimate news about Kamala from being shared? Perhaps because the stories on the website were unflattering positions, and things Kamala had said during her political career. Things that might hurt her chances of becoming the next vice president. Update: as of September 8, 2020, Facebook was no longer preventing the posting of the link mentioned earlier.

Again, just like other news media Facebook is free to engage in these types of practices. However, Facebook cannot simultaneously claim it is simply an unbiased platform, or that the trending news feed is governed by a tool based solely on the topics Facebook users are interested in seeing. At the very least it's an unethical business practice, at worst it's an attempt at social engineering, in reality this type of deceptive editing is probably a little of both. Gizmodo's source claims:

> *"Depending on who was on shift, things would be blacklisted or trending. I'd come on shift and I'd discover that CPAC or Mitt Romney or Glenn Beck or popular conservative topics wouldn't be trending because either the curator didn't recognize the news topic or it was like they had*

a bias against Ted Cruz" - anonymous source,
May 9, 2016 via Gizmodo

One such topic was the scandal involving disgraced IRS director Lois Lerner, who was caught targeting conservative groups in a massive abuse of authority. When the news broke in 2013 that the U.S. Internal Revenue Service had specifically targeted conservative groups applying for tax-exempt status for intense scrutiny. The result of this harassment? Many politically conservative non-profit groups were denied their tax-exempt status, or had their status delayed so they would not be able to effectively participate in the 2012 election cycle. Lerner was forced to address the allegations and went as far as apologizing during a press conference for that conservative groups with the term, 'Tea Party' associated with them had been targeted, along with other conservative groups.

The initial report led to an investigation ordered by the U.S. Department of Justice to be spearheaded by the Federal Bureau of Investigation (which was then under the control of disgraced FBI Director James Comey). The investigation was eventually completed in 2015 and stated that there was, *"...substantial evidence of mismanagement, poor judgment and institutional inertia..."* that all contributed to these targeted audits. The report stopped short of calling the actions criminal, however the FBI Director at the time was James Comey who is alleged to have used his authority for political activism. Why would Facebook actively undermine a trending story? Speculation and conspiracy theorists might leap immediately to covering for the Obama administration, or damage mitigation for the 2014 midterm elections. Likely it was simply to kill a story that had the potential to sway public opinion and give conservative groups a sympathetic look as they struggled against a corrupt government institute.

Regardless, the Gizmodo story gained enough traction that Facebook was forced to respond. A Facebook spokesperson issued this statement:

"We take allegations of bias very seriously. Facebook is a platform for people and perspectives from across the political spectrum. Trending Topics shows you the popular topics and hashtags that are being talked about on Facebook. There are rigorous guidelines in place for the review team to ensure consistency and neutrality. These guidelines do not permit the suppression of political perspectives. Nor do they permit the prioritization of one viewpoint over another or one news outlet over another. These guidelines do not prohibit any news outlet from appearing in Trending Topics."

It's nice that Facebook gave their side of the story and openly declared once more they are an unbiased company, wholly dedicated to preserving all perspectives. However, their actions speak louder than their words. In addition to suppressing stories like the Lois Lerner scandal, Facebook was also artificially promoting the recently coined Black Lives Matter (BLM) movement. The Gizmodo source stated:

"Facebook got a lot of pressure about not having a trending topic for Black Lives Matter. They realized it was a problem, and they boosted it in the ordering. They gave it preference over other topics. When we injected it, everyone started saying, 'Yeah, now I'm seeing it as number one'."

Why would Facebook artificially create a trend for BLM? Because the #BlackLivesMatter movement started on Facebook. From an article published by the Guardian #blacklivesmatter was created by a woman named Patrisse Cullors after reading a post on Facebook written by one of her friends. The article reads:

"Garza's close friend, Patrisse Cullors, read the post in a motel room 300 miles away from

Oakland that same night. Cullors, also a community organiser working in prison reform, started sharing Garza's words with her friends online. She used a hashtag each time she reposted: #blacklivesmatter." - Elizabeth Day, July 19, 2015 via the Guardian

Regardless of a person's individual opinion of BLM as an organization or the words, Black Lives Matter (they do) the fact that Facebook actively created a false trend for it goes against their stated position of a neutral body. Maybe boosting #blacklivesmatter was the right thing to do. Maybe it's important to provide a space for the unheard, the ignored, and the forgotten. Maybe providing that space aligns with Facebook's mission and values. Wouldn't it then also be the right thing for Facebook to stand up and say, "Yes. At Facebook we support #blacklivesmatter and we wanted this topic to trend because BLM is providing a powerful voice for a part of our society that has been ignored for generations. We felt it was the right thing to do." Facebook didn't do that. Why not?

But Gizmodo's sources were anonymous, and for people like me, anonymous sources should be met with skepticism. Thankfully, other sources have come forward, and people have been caught on tape corroborating the Gizmodo story. Once again, Project Veritas broke the story. Published on June 23, 2020 a Project Veritas article released recordings of Facebook content moderator Lara Kontakos making the following statements stating:

"Yeah. I will delete all republicans yeah" – Lara Kontakos via Project Veritas

If someone is wearing a MAGA hat, I am going to delete them for terrorism and just going to like go crazy." - Lara Kontakos via Project Veritas

"If a Trump post was to come up and it was promoting Trump then I can take that down.

Then I would think that, that would be impactful." – Lara Kontakos via Project Veritas

This evidence doesn't confirm the Gizmodo story, but it does sound exactly as their sources described, and provides a chilling look into the culture and practices alive and well within Facebook's content moderation machine.

Regardless of a person's individual political beliefs it should be concerning to everyone when companies like Facebook engage in this type of deceptive practice. Even if someone is a card-carrying member of the communist party and supports every liberal democrat cause, it should be chilling that Facebook is choosing to control what type of information a person can see and interact with. Good ideas always stand on their own and need no misguided attempts at steering people towards them. If Facebook genuinely believes progressive, liberal democrat ideas are the best answers to solve humanity's problems, they absolutely should be advocating for those ideas. They should be helping people understand why those ideas provide the best solutions. They would be wrong, but they would be standing in a far more ethical place. They should not be suppressing information, thoughts, and opinions they disagree with. That's called tyranny. They should also stop pretending to be an unbiased platform. That's called lying.

chapter 7: reddit: the saga of r/the_donald

I would like to note here that despite the actions by CEO Steve Huffman, and some of the blatant actions by the moderators, reddit has done a better job at remaining the least hostile towards free speech and controlling what information people are allowed to engage with. They are by no means unbiased. In fact, only 19% of reddit users self-identify as conservative. The structure of reddit lends itself to creating small communities, and the conservative subreddits that do exist will typically be left to their own devices assuming they follow reddit's general rules and don't step outside the bounds of legality. However there are unsubstantiated rumors regarding Media Matters for America, Shareblue Media, and several other liberal political action groups coordinating in support of the Clinton campaign in 2016 as well as allegations of moderators for various popular forums being paid to drive support for the Clinton campaign.

Of all the allegations, only one has been confirmed with hard evidence. In an email from a Clinton campaign attorney, Correct the Record showed that they were coordinating with the Clinton 2016 campaign. These coordinated actions between Correct the Record and the Clinton 2016 election campaign were allowed by the FEC. Under a rule from 2006, unpaid content posted online isn't regulated by FEC rules. The remaining allegations have only been documented using data observations and observations of rapid and drastic changes in individual moderator behaviours and their approaches to rule enforcement for various subreddits. To date no hard evidence has been produced, and no credible witnesses have stepped forward (an anonymous source did make a rather large accusation, but it too is unsubstantiated). The only supporting evidence documented thus far has been a number of highly suspicious activities.

That being said, this chapter is going to focus around the controversial subreddit r/the_donald, the rise of the popular forum, the actions taken by Steve Huffman (mentioned above) and the lead up to the eventual banning of the subreddit, and it's migration to thedonald.win.

reddit: the front page of the internet. Founded by Steve Huffman and Alexis Ohanian in 2005 reddit is a social media website that aggregates news and stories from around the internet. As of this writing, reddit ranks as the 18th busiest website with over 277 million monthly users, and they remain a privately held company with an estimated revenue of $100 million in 2018. All of the content on reddit is user submitted, meaning the reddit users will create posts containing links, images, or commentary. These posts are organized into user created forums called 'subreddits' and cover just about anything a person can think of including: politics, science, sports, stupid cat videos, video games, people wearing furry costumes, everything. Users can then comment and vote the post up or down. The more up-votes a post receives, the higher ranking it earns in the subreddit. With enough up-votes the post will be placed on reddit's front page.

But it's not a free-for-all, there are guidelines and rules for posting on reddit and users are expected to follow those rules. There are also rules specific to each subreddit. These rules are enforced at two levels. Administrators are paid reddit employees. They deal with high level problems, are representatives of the reddit, and have the authority to remove and promote subreddit moderators. Moderators are the second level of supervision. They are the front-line mediators and are assigned to each subreddit. Moderators are generally volunteering with no technical connection to reddit outside of their moderating duties. There's also a subset of moderators called super moderators. These individuals have moderating oversight over multiple subreddits and are generally friendly with one another. How these moderators and administrators enforce reddit policy and subreddit rule infractions varies. Typically, users who post content that violates the rules will receive a warning or some type of a strike or point. Again, the system for the various subreddits vary, and each subreddit has their own unique consequences when a user steps afoul of the rules that can include muting, suspensions, or even outright banning.

In an ideal world the use of community-based volunteer moderators would create a neutral body of self-governing communities. These communities would be places where ideas are openly shared, and the boundaries of set by reddit are respectfully observed or debated when controversy arose. However, reddit doesn't exist in an ideal world, it exists in the world we live in. That makes reddit just as vulnerable and susceptible to all the faults and flaws prevalent in human society. Enter our antagonists Steve Huffman the CEO and founder of reddit, and r/the_donald, a now banned subreddit. I use the description antagonists for both parties, and the reason(s) should become apparent.

r/the_donald was created in June 2015 shortly after then candidate Donald Trump launched his campaign for the presidency. The intent was to create a place for:

> *"Following the news related to Donald Trump during his presidential run. Media hit pieces from the left and the right will be vetted. Interesting topics include polling, campaign related comments, reactions and push backs."* - r/the_donald

Over the course of the next 5 years, the subreddit grew to nearly 800,000 subscribers and consistently ranked one of the most active and engaged subreddits. To quote Steve Huffman:

> *"there are communities that feel alienated and just want to be heard, and Reddit has always been a place where those voices can be heard"* - Steve Huffman, November 30, 2016

r/the_donald was one of these places. This ability to have a voice was what made the r/the_donald immensely popular. In fact, it was so popular, the users were so excited to support President Trump, by 2016 posts from the forum were often up voted enough to make reddit's front page. This was a problem for reddit, not because of what r/the_donald was, but because of the politics that drove its success. This popularity immediately drew the ire of the orange man bad gang and in December of 2015, users from liberal forums began to engage in a practice called brigading. Brigading is when a group of individuals are coordinated together in an effort to harass another group or individual. It's typically frowned upon in forums such as reddit. This targeted harassment only served to embolden the users at r/the_donald. They took it as a challenge that liberals had invaded their space, with the sole intention of harassing them simply for their political beliefs. These attacks continued and did not have the desired effect. By February of 2016 r/the_donald had grown to over 10,000 subscribers. This coincided with then candidate Trump's rise in popularity among voters which also accelerated the forum's growth. By the end of February r/the_donald had reached 40,000 subscribers.

February had also seen posts from r/the_donald trending four separate times which was phenomenal for a subreddit that size. As a comparison r/politics has more than 6 million subscribers and is one of the more popular subreddits. r/the_donald had been able to achieve this notoriety because of the way the reddit trending algorithm worked at the time. There was a time-based weighting factor that started as soon as a new post was created. Posts that received a large number of up votes within a certain time period would begin to trend and show up on r/all. This allowed posts made in r/the_donald to trend with fewer overall votes, because the posts had been favored for trending due to this time-based factor. Once these posts began to trend, they gained even more traction on the r/all. This exposure created more exposure to a larger audience who could then add additional up votes, and because r/all is much larger than r/the_donald the posts that were able to trend here gave more exposure for r/the_donald. Of course, this popularity led to more brigading by liberal users, and all of these things combined created a feedback loop contributing to r/the_donald's continued growth.

Enter Milo Yiannopoulos. Infamous or famous, Milo is or was a popular ultra conservative personality from

Britain. His support for President Trump, and popularity lead him to participate in a reddit event known as an AMA or ask me anything on March 1, 2016. This added to the accelerating growth r/the_donald was experiencing, and the subreddit ended the day with 47,123 subscribers. The ever-expanding pool of subscribers primarily consisted of Donald Trump supporters, and liberal agitators there to cause trouble. This trend continued, and minor spats between users became the standard fare for any typical day. Then on June 12, 2016 a tragic event occured. The Orlando nightclub shooting. People were shocked. People were angry. People were sad. And all those people were looking for a space to talk about such a horrific event. A space where they could discuss the emotion of it all, openly, honestly, and brutally sometimes. Many turned to their favorite subreddits looking for news, new details, and to share their thoughts and prayers for the victims. Yet during this tragedy, for some reason posts and comments people were sharing were being removed by moderators of the r/news subreddit. Once people realized what was happening, they were furious.

But it wasn't just the user's fury they faced. The moderators of r/news had underestimated how negatively the users would react to their censorship campaign. This heavy-handed censorship had consequences, and it led to more than 85,000 subscribers fleeing r/news. Many users who left r/news sought refuge in forums that allowed more open discussions to take place. r/the_donald was one such place, and out of frustration, and perhaps out of spite, users flocked there. r/the_donald gained over 11,000 subscribers in a single day, and posts from their forum were featured in more than half of the top 25 posts on r/all. This event became a tipping point for reddit. The popularity of r/the_donald could not be allowed and so the orange man bad gang mobilized. Three days later, on June 15, 2020 reddit changed the way it's trending algorithm worked. CEO Steve Huffman announced the change to the algorithm that helped populate r/all and in an email, Huffman wrote:

"We have seen many communities like r/the_donald over the years; ones that attempt to dominate the conversation on Reddit at the expense of everyone else. This undermines Reddit, and we are not going to allow it." – Steve Huffman, June 16, 2016

The change had the desired effect. Posts from r/the_donald went from appearing on r/all regularly, to only a few posts a week trend enough to reach the popular subreddit. It's this clamp down on popular and trending information that becomes troubling. When a CEO changes the rules mid game to prevent a political viewpoint or candidate from being seen or heard it stamps out freedom of speech and open debate. Huffman's actions here demonstrate reddit's willingness to stifle uncomfortable speech, but reddit had previously admitted they were willing to do so. Flashback to 2015. In a growing response to community outcry, reddit began to ban certain categories of content. This included things like creepy pictures of women in public, or revenge porn. At the time revenge porn was a rising problem being addressed by the U.S. court system. reddit took the lead and decided to ban it outright. Of course, these bans caused a stir among the reddit user base with accusations that the company had sold out and was no longer a safe harbor for free speech. In a statement given as a response to the backlash, Huffman wrote:

"Neither Alexis nor I created reddit to be a bastion of free speech, but rather as a place where open and honest discussion can happen" - Steve Huffman, July 14, 2015

But this wasn't always reddit's official position. In fact, it was during a Forbes interview in 2012, that Alexis Ohanian was asked how the Founding Fathers might have reacted to reddit. Ohanian' response was that he viewed it as exactly that when he stated:

"a bastion of free speech on the World Wide Web? I bet they would like it" - Alexis Ohanian, February 2, 2012

Huffman's claim also contradicts other past CEO's. For example, in 2012 former reddit CEO Yishan Wong wrote in a memo to reddit employees, *"we stand for free speech"*. Huffman's proclamation sounds closer to former interim (and unpopular) CEO Ellen Pao. She had similar sentiments as Huffman, and in an interview given to NPR had this to say:

> *"The question is whether it would make them fear for their safety, or the safety of those around them or where it makes them feel like it's not a safe platform. Somebody expressing ideas that aren't consistent with everybody's views is something that we encourage. There are certain posts that do make people feel unsafe, that people feel threatened or they feel that their family or friends or people near them are going to be unsafe, and those are the specific things that we are focused on today. It's not our site's goal to be a completely free speech platform. We want to be a safe platform and we want to be a platform that also protects privacy at the same time."* - Ellen Pao, May 19, 2015

But that's to be expected, as time's change, companies change and reddit has made it clear they are moving towards sanitization as they seek to draw in more advertisers. What's more important to recognize, and Ellen Pao was correct when she said that ideas that aren't consistent with everybody's views is something reddit would encourage. Without saying it directly, Ellen Pao was defending diversity of thought here. Diversity of thought is crucial to innovate and develop solutions to the challenges that face humanity. This outlook must have changed under

Huffman as he moved to diminish the voice of people who supported President Trump and silence their dissent.

On July 27, 2016 then candidate Donald Trump stepped into the feud directly. He participated in an AMA hosted by r/the_donald. Much like the rest of the Trump 2016 campaign, it broke tradition by doing so. Most celebrity AMA's are hosted in r/IAmA. President Obama had participated in an AMA in 2012, and it was hosted by r/IAmA. Apparently, President Trump felt it was important to work directly with his supporters and buck this trend. Questions were submitted by r/the_donald users, and President Trump answered. Below are some of the selected questions and responses.

> ***Question:*** *How will you, as president, tackle this protected class of media elites without stepping on the first amendment rights of average Americans?*

> ***President Trump:*** *"I have been very concerned about media bias and the total dishonesty of the press. I think new media is a great way to get out the truth."*

> ***Question:*** *Will you curb H-1B abuse and make sure visas are going to people who want to become American, stay American, and make America great?*

> ***President Trump:*** *"I have put forward a detailed plan for H-1B reform to protect American workers which can be viewed on the immigration paper on my website. My plan is the exact opposite of Crooked Hillary Clinton."*

> ***Question:*** *What will you do as President to ensure that myself and others can not only enjoy the security of having health insurance, but also afford to keep it?*

President Trump: *"One of the first things I will do is to repeal and replace disastrous Obamacare. I will put forward an amazing new plan, which will include many reforms, such as letting people buy insurance across state lines, increasing choice and competition, and bargaining for better, cheaper drug prices."*

Question: *What would say to a young college student like myself who is considering a job in law enforcement, but might have been discouraged by the recent attacks on police?*

President Trump: *"We will always stand with and support our nation's amazing police. There is nothing more honorable than serving your community and your country as a law enforcement officer. My administration will protect those who protect us. Thank you to all the incredible police officers in our country tonight."*

Question: *We firmly believe Hillary will try and steal this election through vote fraud, especially given recent events. What is your campaign doing to ensure that we have a fair election?*

President Trump: *"Voter fraud is always a serious concern and authorities must be vigilant from keeping those from voting that are not authorized to do so."*

Question: *"What is the most important thing you would like to convey about yourself and your policy positions to the people who voted for Bernie in the primary but are now considering either staying home or voting third party in November?"*

President Trump: *"Though Bernie is exhausted and has given up on his revolution, many of his voters still want to keep up the fight. I expect that millions of Bernie voters will refuse to vote for Hillary because of her support for the War in Iraq, the invasion of Libya, NAFTA and TPP, and of course because she is totally bought and sold by special interests. She and her husband have been paid millions and millions by global corporations and powerful interests who will control her every decision. She is their puppet, and they pull the strings. We welcome with open arms all voters who want an honest government and to fix our rigged system so it works for the people. This includes fixing one of Bernie's biggest issues, our terrible trade deals that strip our country of its jobs and wealth."*

Question: *"Mr. Trump, what do you feel is the greatest issue facing young Americans today?"*

President Trump: *"The question most young people ask me is about the rising cost of education, terrible student debt and total lack of jobs. Youth unemployment is through the roof, and millions more are underemployed. It's a total disaster! I will create millions of new jobs, reform our education system, and work to free young Americans from the awful burden of debt."*

Question: *"So my question to you is, what do you say to people like me who are on the fence about voting 3rd party(Johnson/Stein) or for you?"*

President Trump: *"Americans in every party are tired of our rigged system and corrupt*

*politicians and want to reform our government
so it no longer benefits the powerful at the
expense of everyone else. They know I will fix it
so it works for them and their families. Hillary
Clinton's message is that things will never
change. My message is that things have to
change, and they have to change right now. We
have to change a foreign policy that has led us
to one economic disaster after another, and an
economic policy that has failed our poorest
citizens. We will never fix a rigged system by
relying on the people who rigged it in the first
place. I am going to return the government to
the people. Together, we will Make America
Great Again."*

Most of the questions he answered were from the r/the_donald regulars which at the time included Milo Yiannopoulos. There were some irrelevant and cheerleader questions not included here, but overall, not a bad AMA. It gave President Trump the opportunity to use a press conference style approach, and still reach out directly to his supporters in the digital space. It was heavily moderated due to the targeted harassment by liberal users there to cause trouble. Many comments were deleted during the AMA as the moderators had previously warned users they would be doing. The AMA ended, and shortly after President Trump landed in Toledo for a rally. Conversation between users commenting on the AMA thread continued, and Trump supporters seemed happy with the outcome. In particular, the regular users in r/the_donald were excited President Trump had taken the time to engage with them. However, the up-vote numbers don't necessarily reflect that. It was noted by observers that President Trump's AMA thread had a significant number of down votes. When Obama participated in an AMA the thread was mostly up voted. Some people will say this indicates how unpopular President Trump is. Other people will say this is evidence that proves liberal agitators were actively brigading the r/the_donald event. But remember the small 19%

conservative user base reddit has? The lopsided demographics may be the root cause here, but it's probably a little bit of all three contributing.

After President Trump's successful AMA, the 2016 campaign continued, and regardless of the changes implemented by reddit to stifle the popularity of r/the_donald, the community continued to grow, and the forum's popularity continued to rise. By November 7, the day before the 2016 election, r/the_donald had grown to 267,342 subscribers. As the forum grew, so did the number of voices and opinions, and as with all things on the internet, some of the posts began to go off the rails. Moderators did their best to enforce the rules, which created an ever-increasing tension between users and moderators. But with over 250,000 users it was difficult to track down everything.

Imagine having to read the class notes for 250,000 people. That's what it was like, only the internet never turns off and it was a 24/7 game of cat and mouse. reddit administrators used this to continually cite r/the_donald for policy infractions. These infractions became a source of continual frustration for reddit, and particularly CEO Steve Huffman. So much so that what he did next is frankly embarrassing for him. He abused his authority as CEO when he edited user comments that criticized and insulted him. In what subreddit? r/the_donald. Keep in mind here he is a 32 almost 33-year-old man, not some acne faced kid. He's CEO to a company valued at nearly $1 billion dollars. And he used his power as CEO to anonymously change user comments that referenced his username, u/spez, to instead say the usernames of moderators of r/the_donald that he didn't like. Why? Pettiness. Lack of leadership ability. Frustration. Honestly, who knows. I doubt even Huffman knows. Humans have a knack for doing things they cannot explain in retrospect. Once caught though Huffman did own up to his mistake, kind of. Even if he didn't apologize to r/the_donald directly, he did issue an apology, kind of, to the entire reddit community. The first part of it reads:

"Hi All,

I am sorry: I am sorry for compromising the trust you all have in Reddit, and I am sorry to those that I created work and stress for, particularly over the holidays. It is heartbreaking to think that my actions distracted people from their family over the holiday; instigated harassment of our moderators; and may have harmed Reddit itself, which I love more than just about anything.

The United States is more divided than ever, and we see that tension within Reddit itself. The community that was formed in support of President-elect Donald Trump organized and grew rapidly, but within it were users that devoted themselves to antagonising the broader Reddit community.

Many of you are aware of my attempt to troll the trolls last week. I honestly thought I might find some common ground with that community by meeting them on their level. It did not go as planned. I restored the original comments after less than an hour, and explained what I did.

I spent my formative years as a young troll on the Internet. I also led the team that built Reddit ten years ago, and spent years moderating the original Reddit communities, so I am as comfortable online as anyone. As CEO, I am often out in the world speaking about how Reddit is the home to conversation online, and a follow on question about harassment on our site is always asked. We have dedicated many of our resources to fighting harassment on Reddit, which is why letting one of our most engaged communities openly harass me felt hypocritical.

While many users across the site found what I did funny, or appreciated that I was standing up to the bullies (I received plenty of support from users of r/the_donald), many others did not. I understand what I did has greater implications than my relationship with one community, and it is fair to raise the question of whether this erodes trust in Reddit. I hope our transparency around this event is an indication that we take matters of trust seriously. Reddit is no longer the little website my college roommate, u/kn0thing, and I started more than eleven years ago. It is a massive collection of communities that provides news, entertainment, and fulfillment for millions of people around the world, and I am continually humbled by what Reddit has grown into. I will never risk your trust like this again, and we are updating our internal controls to prevent this sort of thing from happening in the future." - Steve Huffman, November 30, 2016

It's a little long, but I thought it was important to share here directly because this section of his apology for his abuse of power is indicative of his combative attitude, and growing frustration towards r/the_donald. For the people that couldn't make it past the second paragraph when Steve blames the users in r/the_donald for his actions let me summarize. He apologizes for his actions, then blames reddit users and r/the_donald. He talks about the election and how magnanimous he is for allowing the miscreants in r/the_donald to exist on reddit at all. He promises to never do something like that again. He threatens to ban users, moderators, and entire subreddits. The remaining quarter of his half apology eventually ends with two announcements. One being that he enabled filtering for r/all. This will allow users to skip over posts from specific subreddits, and the second is disallowing certain posts from r/the_donald to make it to r/all. As punishment for his abuse of power. An interesting for of apology. But that is his right as the CEO, I'm just reminded of the phrase, power doesn't corrupt, it magnifies.

The saga doesn't end there. As a reminder the story has only made it to November of 2016. For those not keeping track it's been a about a year and half since r/the_donald was created and in that time they have: wrought the wrath of the reddit CEO, caused reddit to alter its trending algorithm, hosted a presidential candidate AMA breaking a long standing tradition, caused a rule change for stickied posts (posts that are pinned to the top of the subreddit feed), and forced the CEO to add a filtering option for one of the most popular subreddits r/all. If I'm keeping score, a subreddit that only hit 300,000 followers on November 25, 2016 is punching way over its weight class.

In March 2017 things flared up again after reddit showed r/the_donald as having over six million subscribers, rather than the 385,000 or so displayed on the live counter. reddit was forced to respond, and Anna Soellner, a Director of Communications for reddit released this statement:

> *"When we released the new ads self-serve product yesterday, the ad interface said subscribers in the targeting dropdown list. However, the actual number represented here was not subscribers, but was actually daily unique visitors to the subreddit."* – Anna Soellner, March 31, 2017 via FoxNews

reddit's assertion was that these numbers were simply a typo. The advertising page was meant to say r/the_donald averaged 6 million unique visitors each day with 385,000 subscribers. Anna went on to say the error has been partly fixed by Friday. Most likely true, but wouldn't that imply the fix would be as simple as well? Why only a partial fix? Transposing numbers into the incorrect column or referencing the wrong drop-down list should be as simple as swapping pointers. Technology may be to blame here. reddit was rewritten in a coding language called python in 2005, and in 2008 python released version 3.0 (current version) which was not entirely backward compatible with 2.0 versions. Regardless of the actual cause for the number error, the controversy only helped to further strain the relationship between reddit and r/the_donald with one side claiming innocence and the other screaming foul play.

By May 1, 2017 r/the_donald had only achieved around 390,000 subscribers. Its growth had slowed and had not been without setbacks as the friction between reddit and r/the_donald had only increased. Both moderators and paid reddit administrators being frustrated by the perceived behaviours across the aisle. reddit, for their part struggled with balancing r/the_donald's popularity and engagement, and their desire to control the narrative surrounding President Trump. The moderators were frustrated with the seemingly endless rule changes and inequitable enforcement that seemed to target and harass r/the_donald directly. Then on May 19, 2017 reddit launched a ban campaign against r/the_donald. Without warning, three long time moderators were removed by reddit administrators who provided this message to the remaining moderators:

> *"Hey mods, we want to provide an update on the situation that has been ongoing since yesterday. We have removed OhSnapYouGotServed, JesusWoreNikeSlides and henny, as moderators for failing to comply with the additional rules we previously communicated. They are not allowed to be added back to the mod team here under these or any other account names. The rule violations are fostering an environment of threats and harassment towards users, and antagonism towards other communities, and, as you've*

*been repeatedly told, this is not welcome on the
site. We welcome communicating with you
directly and we can work towards making this
a healthy community together. Thank you, the
reddit admin team."*

In response, the remaining admins decided to set
r/the_donald to private and post this message:

*"reddit removed three The_Donald mods
because we refused to comply by a special set
of rules that were solely imposed on this
subreddit to marginalize the only major
community which doesn't conform to the echo
chamber of reddit and corporate media. Our
mod team continues to stand strong in support
of free speech, equal treatment and application
of the rules for all subreddits. We are
temporarily private in a show of strength
against these unfair and unequal rules."*

What rules did r/the_donald violate that the
moderators felt they were being inequitably punished for?
Allegations of violating harassment policies surrounding the
practice of brigading. According to some these policies
weren't being equally applied to liberal leaning subreddit
moderators, including moderators from the counter
subreddit, r/enoughtrumpspam or ETS. In fact, according
to Steve Huffman, they were only being applied to
r/the_donald. In a statement given shortly after admitting
to editing posts made by r/the_donald users months
earlier, Huffman was asked if the rule changes reddit would
be implementing would be site wide policies. He replied:

*"Right now, just [r/the_donald]. Going forward,
we'll just take away their toys specifically and
move on."* – Steve Huffman, December 2, 2016
via FoxNews

These bans did have some unintended consequences. The attention r/the_donald gained from the ensuing controversy resulted in an increase of nearly 13,000 subscribers over the next 4 days. This 4-day surge in subscribers outpaced the entire previous 30-day total.

Then in July 2017 controversy rose once again from r/the_donald. President Trump tweeted out a meme that had been posted by a reddit user at r/the_donald. The meme featured a short video clip of President Trump from one of his WWE appearances in 2007. In the clip, it shows President Trump in a fight with Vince McMahon where he is choking Vince. However, in the meme version, the creator had superimposed the CNN logo over Vince's face. It was a meme meant to represent President Trump taking down CNN as a fake news media outlet. As metaphors go, it was a fairly accurate depiction of the ongoing Trump vs. CNN feud. It's 2020 and the antagonistic reporters for the orange man bad gang still haven't figured out how to handle President Trump, and it's getting worse for them. Watching Press Secretary Kayleigh McEnany smash reporters is like watching Mike Tyson fight a baby.

Back to the story though, shortly after President Trump's tweet of the short clip, a firestorm ensued. The reddit user issued an apology after CNN implied, they would dox the original meme creator. Doxxing is a practice of exposing private personal information about someone to the general public. It's generally considered poor taste, and is a practice typically frowned upon. In a statement issued after the reddit user issued their apology CNN feeds their loyal followers with diatribe that won't be included here, and ends by giving this ominous warning:

> *"CNN reserves the right to publish his identity should any of that change."* - CNN, July 5, 2017

#CNNblackmail becoming a trending topic on Twitter, and in r/the_donald.

About a month later, things would turn ugly. On August 11, 2017 white nationalists invaded Charlottesville,

Virginia (which was where Steve Huffman attended college). The personal connection was too much for the CEO, and I don't blame him. In his 2018 interview with the New Yorker Steve recalls telling his team:

> *"If any of these people are on reddit, I want them gone. Nuke 'em"* - Steve Huffman, March 19, 2018

At the time reddit's rules explicitly prohibited content that encouraged or incited violence. But that rule was only four words long and this incident exposed a potential gap. Some reddit users, including some users in r/the_donald, were celebrating the death of a young woman who was participating in a counter protest. She had been run over by a white supremacist in a horrific attack. They say every rule exists because of some asshole, and it was certainly true in this case. reddit was once again forced to change its rules (and the rule has been further updated) to now read:

> *Do not post content that encourages, glorifies, incites, or calls for violence or physical harm against an individual or a group of people; likewise, do not post content that glorifies or encourages the abuse of animals. We understand there are sometimes reasons to post violent content (e.g., educational, newsworthy, artistic, satire, documentary, etc.) so if you're going to post something violent in nature that does not violate these terms, ensure you provide context to the viewer so the reason for posting is clear.*

While there are exceptions to this rule as stated, reddit users would no longer be allowed to glorify a woman being run over by car. This was a positive change for the reddit as a whole.

After the Charlottesville incident, things returned to status quo over the next few months. New rules governing posting and commenting behaviours were enforced regularly against users at the r/the_donald. While the subreddit r/the_donald had trended nearly 50 times in 2016, through 2017 that number was cut in half. Minor flare ups occurred between moderators and reddit administrators with accusations still flying both ways. reddit admins claiming the r/the_donald was violating rules, and moderators claiming reddit isn't enforcing rules equitably and targeting r/the_donald users and moderators for harassment. Neither side had done much to dispel those accusations.

In March 2018 things intensified again after Steve Huffman gave an interview to the New Yorker. During the interview Huffman tells the reporter:

> *"I'm confident that reddit could sway elections.*
> *We wouldn't do it, of course. And I don't know*
> *how many times we could get away with it.*
> *But, if we really wanted to, I'm sure Reddit*
> *could have swayed at least this election, this*
> *once."* – Steve Huffman, March 12, 2018 via
> the New Yorker

This stirred the pot even more for users at r/the_donald as it had been a long held conspiracy theory that reddit, amongst other tech companies had colluded to interfere in the 2016 election, and there were fears they would double down on their efforts heading into the 2020 election in an effort to prevent a second term for President Trump. Huffman's statement only served to stoke those fears. It was the counter cry to the liberal media narratives of election interference. Liberals peddled their Russian bot theories, and the r/the_donald was convinced Silicon Valley was plotting to steal 2020. r/the_donald sought to push back anyway they could. Overall, the moderators did a good job at weeding out instigators and agitators, but as always reddit had given them a herculean task and there were continual warnings.

For the next year, the subreddit continued to grow and by June 1, 2019 r/the_donald had more than 745,000 subscribers. The feud between moderators and reddit administrators had also continued to grow. More accusations, more rule enforcements until June 26, 2019 things finally came to a head. reddit had finally seen enough and decided to quarantine r/the_donald. This meant that the subreddit wouldn't be visible in normal searches unless you were a subscriber. This would mean r/the_donald's organic growth potential would be severely limited. The reason for the quarantine was explained by reddit in a message sent to the moderator team:

> *Dear Mods,*
>
> *We want to let you know that your community has been quarantined, as outlined in reddit's content policy.*
>
> *The reason for the quarantine is that over the last few months we have observed repeated rule-breaking behavior in your community and an over-reliance on reddit admins to manage users and remove posts that violate our content policy, including content that encourages or incites violence. Most recently, we have observed this behavior in the form of encouragement of violence towards police officers and public officials in Oregon. This is not only in violation of our site-wide policies, but also your own community rules (rule #9). You can find violating content that we removed in your mod logs.*
>
> *As we have discussed in the past, and as detailed in our content policy and moderator guidelines, we expect you to enforce against rule-breaking content. You've made progress over the last year, but we continue to observe and take action on a disproportionate amount of rule-breaking behavior in this community. We recognize that you do remove posts that are reported, but we are troubled that violent*

content more often goes unreported, and worse, is upvoted.

User reports and downvotes are an essential way that reddit functions to moderate content. Limiting or prohibiting them prevents you from moderating your community effectively. Because of this, we are disabling your custom styling in order to restore these essential functions.

It's good that reddit administrators were identifying these types of violent posts. Despite claims that reddit was a bastion of free speech, they clearly had amended their rules to carve out things that could make people fear for their physical safety. This is reflected in not only the continuously updating policies, but also as a general strategy put forth by reddit's leadership team, as well as reddit's founders. Which is why I'm glad reddit quarantined the r/the_donald for the following user comments made about public officials in Oregon:

"Let's hunt them for sport! And televise it!."- neoaikon, June 25, 2019.

"This should be grounds for immediate execution, just like in the military." - Pinhead_Cotton, June 25, 2019.

"...the only way to deal with these people is killing them..." - StonecrusherCarnifex, June 25, 2019.

"Shoot these fuckers. In the knees. For running like pieces of shit." - titanicx, June 25, 2019.

"They crossed state lines, can the FBI go Waco on them?" - drillosuar, June 25, 2019.

Only these comments weren't made in r/the_donald. These comments were made by users in r/politics. The list of comments made by people attacking GOP politicians is much, much longer, but the point is made, users in the subreddit r/politics were making violent threats against the same Oregon public officials the reddit administrators had mentioned in their letter, and about the same news topic. Only reddit didn't apply their rules equally to r/politics. That's why these comments were identified in a report released in August 2019. In it the authors identified hundreds of similar comments made in liberal leaning subreddits as a direct response to reddit's actions to quarantine r/the_donald.

In the report the authors note that the quarantine was put into place on the first day of the Democratic primary debates. Once again fueling the question on how far Steve Huffman, and reddit are willing to go to influence the election after his comments from 2018. In the report the authors note that the quarantine for r/the_donald was tied to several user comments on a post regarding republican legislators in Oregon fleeing to prevent a quorum, and divisive vote on a bill regarding climate change. This further evidences the political bias within reddit, and demonstrates their attempt to stifle dissent from liberal narratives. The report further accuses reddit administrators of failing to act in good faith. They highlight the differences in the way reddit rules and policies are enforced against r/the_donald by noting that:

> *"...in all other known instances of a subreddit being placed in quarantine, administrators first contact subreddit moderators to discuss content believed to be in violation of Reddit's site-wide policies and an opportunity is given to remediate the situation. No such courtesy was afforded to r/the_donald."*

The report also calls out several other subreddits for violent comments and content posted by users, specifically the anti-police subreddit, r/bad_cop_no_donut. The report identified over 40 comments made by users that directly called for the murder or execution of law enforcement officials, yet no quarantine was issued against this subreddit.

By October 2019, when the quarantine for r/the_donald still hadn't been lifted, U.S. Congressional Representative Jim Banks authored an open letter to reddit. In it, he does not mince words stating:

> *"Although the initial imposition of the quarantine may have been justified, its continuation in the face of r/the_donald's compliance with sitewide content policies and ahead of the 2020 election amounts to ideologically motivated election interference. To this point, the same content-policy violations that led to r/The_Donald's quarantine take place regularly and egregiously in numerous left-wing subreddits."* – Jim Banks, October 22, 2019

Representative Banks is correct when he states that the same content policy violations are not disciplined the same across the liberal leaning subreddits. The comments shared earlier clearly demonstrate this. The interesting take away is when Banks mentions election interference. Later in his letter, Representative Banks specifically mentions the New Yorker interview from 2018 where Huffman brags reddit would be able to sway the election. Whether or not Huffman believed what he said or if reddit was even capable of doing so, Huffman said it, and now there was direct evidence reddit had taken action to do so. Quarantining the largest subreddit for conservative voices the day the democratic debates is taking place certainly had a negative impact on a community of over 700,000 people. The quarantine would directly undermine their ability to comment on and refute claims made by the nominees. The quarantine would hamper the ability to share policy histories and voting records for the democratic politicians vying to be the next president of the United States. Even if that doesn't meet the legal standard for election interference, it certainly is interfering in the election. When reddit quarantined r/the_donald they definitely showed that reddit was willing and able to use its power to sway an election, even if it only had the impact of a slight breeze.

The next day reddit responded to the quarantine appeal submitted by r/the_donald moderators: a resounding no. The moderators at r/the_donald released the explanation reddit provided. It was a long winded, non-specific response in which they claim:

> *"…your subscribers continue to upvote violative content at a significantly higher rate than subreddits of a similar size and topical focus to yours, in line with the figures we see in other quarantined subreddits, across the political spectrum."*

reddit also claims they're not able to release the methodology they use, and so no quantitative analysis can be done to show if what they are asking is even achievable. The message seems to imply moderators of r/the_donald are being asked to police more than 700,000 users across the entire reddit platform, and not just within r/the_donald.

In November 2019, the impeachment circus for President Trump was in full swing. News broke of the potential identity for the whistleblower who was the key to the entire democratic case. As this was a newsworthy story, much of reddit was in heated debate and discussion around the impeachment. reddit made it very clear in a statement released by their spokesperson:

> *"Our policy encourages an open discussion regarding issues of public and political relevance, however it forbids posting of personal information, or the encouragement of harassment or vigilantism."* – reddit, November 20, 2019 via CNN

In a spat over news of the whistleblower, reddit administrators issued a warning, and alleged that the administrators had to remove dozens of posts inviting vigilantism and harassment, and to remove posts that were nothing but attempts at bringing mob attention to the suspected whistleblower. In response the moderators claim no such posts were created, stating that no content posted in r/the_donald was of a harassing nature, encouraged vigilantism, or intended to bring mob attention to the whistleblower. Instead the moderators claimed the administrators were conflating comments made by users in r/the_donald simply identifying the whistleblower with harassment so they could once again target r/the_donald for harassment, and inequitable enforcement of reddit's own stated policies. This was the last straw for several members of the moderator team.

Sometime around November 21, 2019, shortly after being threatened by reddit, a team of moderators decided to launch a new home for r/the_donald with a website: thedonald.win. Setup in a similar forum type format, registered users were finally free of harassment by the orange man bad gang, and their liberal minded administrators of reddit. In a few days thedonald.win had registered thousands of individuals looking for a conservative home and respite from the liberal bias that permeated most of the digital world. Their message is simple:

> *"Welcome to the forum of choice for The President of The United States, Donald Trump! Be advised this forum is for serious supporters of President Trump. We have discussions, memes, AMAs, and more. We are not politically correct."*

The story doesn't end there. Even with their new home, moderators and subscribers at r/the_donald were determined to remain active and stand in defiance of the ever-increasing liberal echo chamber constructed by the orange man bad gang. In February of 2020, reddit issued another blow to r/the_donald. reddit administrators removed half of r/the_donald moderators, and in the same month Steve Huffman announced reddit would also begin enforcing a policy that punished users for up voting content that violated reddit's policies. Under the new rule users can be suspended for simply up voting a post of comment that reddit deems inappropriate. The trouble is this oftentimes comes down to interpretation. To quote reddit here, context matters, and the context of some content is often open to interpretation. Per the rules of reddit users are not allowed to glorify violence. Does that mean a reddit user can neither post nor up vote content in support of Kurdish Yazidi women who formed a militia unit to protect themselves from brutal ISIS terror attacks and enslavement? These fearsome fighters certainly killed people while defending their lives and their families. Not only should they be supported for their actions, their bravery should be glorified. Context matters, as does the mindset of who is judging these comments and posts. Based on the administrators past biased actions in stifling conservative thought it seems this rule would unduly impact someone that views the world through a conservative lens.

By May of 2020, during the height of the covid-19 panic, even congress had enough. Five U.S. Congressional Representatives penned an open letter to reddit once more. On May 28, 2020, Jim Banks, Matt Gaetz, Ted Budd, Ted Yoho, and Jody Hice all signed a letter condemning reddit's actions and interference in the 2020 election. They cite inequitable enforcement of reddit policy noting that not only do other subreddits frequently violate policies, but in one egregious comment a moderator for r/thedrumpf posted that they would like to have people who support President Trump drink arsenic. They add similar apparent policy violations and point out that these users were not subject to the same penalties as moderators and subscribers for r/the_donald. Again, they cite the 2018 interview where Huffman claims reddit could sway the election, and again point out that by selectively enforcing reddit policy against conservative voices, reddit is in fact swaying the election.

Unfortunately, the congressmen's letter would fall onto deaf ears. Nearly one month later, on June 29, 2020 reddit would formally ban r/the_donald ending 5 years of frustration and fighting. While reddit was able to create a large enough tangle of rules and hurdles to silence the conservative safe haven on reddit, winning the war, it may have been a pyrrhic victory. r/the_donald created a firestorm of controversy during its tenure on reddit. r/the_donald forced the CEO to alter the trending rules multiple times, elicited Steve Huffman's inner troll to burst out into the public light demonstrating his true character (power magnifies, it doesn't corrupt), and highlighted the true nature of digital technology companies: a grotesque willingness to sacrifice their founding core values on the altar of virtue signaling, to orange man bad gang.

chapter 8: no ma'amazon

Amazon is not so much a social media platform as it is a digital reseller crossed with a bazaar. Whereas Ebay would be closer to a digital flea market, Amazon seems to strike a balance between online retail, consignment sales, and digital storefront mall. Of all the digital tech companies it is least like a publisher in both function and format. Their attempts at social engineering are more benign (if it ever can be) but they are slowing stepping into the role as arbiters of morality. Amazon's ever-increasing attempts to become the retail branch of thought control came to my attention when they announced they were halting sales of confederate flags on their platform.

This announcement came just a few days after a crazed mass murderer killed 9 black congregates at the Emanuel African Methodist Episcopal Church on June 17, 2015. The perpetrator was a white supremacist who had co-opted the confederate flag as a symbol of his hateful ideology, as many similar racists do. It's certainly a nice sentiment to remove something many people find offensive and hurtful, but Amazon's announcement, and their political theatrics rang a bit hollow. Corporations that chase 'social justice' issues should be met with skepticism. I say this because it's usually just for social credit points, and not for any actual moral boundaries. To highlight this, as of September 23, 2020 Amazon is still selling the following items: confederate flag masks, confederate flag women's shorts, the Mississippi state flag that previously featured the confederate flag, confederate flag pillows, and confederate flag blankets. And that's just the first 3 pages of results when doing a search for confederate.

Regardless immediately after I learned of Amazon's decision, I went to Amazon.com and browsed for Rhodesian flags. It was not surprising that there were numerous of these flags still for sale. For clarity, Rhodesia was the internationally condemned, and essentially apartheid state of modern-day Zimbabwe. The founders of Rhodesia sought independence and white controlled minority rule after

Britain began decolonizing the region. They weren't exactly champions of equal rights. Why is this relevant to the story? The murderer who perpetrated this awful crime was an American. What does this have to do with a defunct nation in Africa?

Without going too far into the heaping garbage pile that is white supremacist ideology, the Rhodesian flag is another co-opted symbol these human turds like to wave about. It's relevant here because the piece of human garbage who killed nine people in Charleston that tragic day was also wearing the Rhodesian flag. If Amazon was genuinely concerned about stemming racism by removing racist iconography, then the Rhodesian flag should also be removed from their marketplace. Since then it appears Amazon has applied some logical consistency in their decision making. A brief search turned up no results for a Rhodesian flag, and instead will recommend the Zimbabwe flag as an alternative product. Although a Rhodesian patch did show up, in Amazon's defense it was tagged as an old-style Zimbabwe patch. It'll be interesting to see what my Amazon recommendations are after doing that five minutes of research.

As a private business, their right to sell, or refuse to sell certain items should be respected. If someone is that ruffled by Amazon not selling a confederate battle flag, they have every right to start a competing platform that will sell every ounce of confederate memorabilia. Best of luck. It just seems a bit suspicious when a company as ubiquitous as Amazon begins regulating what a person can and cannot buy based on some notion of what is and is not moral. Obviously, Amazon is bound by law to not sell anything illegal or regulated beyond the scope of their business service. This means, sadly, Amazon doesn't sell cocaine, machine guns, pangolins, or hookers. Not yet anyway. The question then becomes this: is Amazon morally obligated to stop selling confederate flags? The only people qualified to answer that question are the senior leaders at Amazon. I won't speculate on where they should or should not draw that line. Again, what is concerning is how Amazon arrives at the decision on where to draw those lines. Maybe

Amazon is genuinely guided by a moral principle to remove certain items to combat racism. Based on the confederate products still readily available on Amazon, that decision does not appear to be the case.

Even if it was, and Amazon let their ethical boundaries drive their business decisions, is that Amazon's role as a company? If not, then who are the gatekeepers for what is, and is not considered racist? 100 years ago, addressing a black person as a negro would have been considered polite, given the alternative many democrats used. Today the use of that term would probably get a person fired. They would be labeled a racist, condemned on social media, and brow beaten into issuing an apology. But would it be racist? According to liberals all of the following things are racist:

> *"How dogs help keep multiracial neighborhoods socially segregated"* - Naomi Schalit, May 22, 2019 via The Conversation

> *"Math is racist: How data is driving inequality"* - Aimee Rawlins, September 6, 2016 via CNN

> *"Illinois Rep Wants to Abolish History Classes as Racist"* - Mike Shedlock, August 3, 2020 via The Street

> *"Coffee shop racism: where America's racial divisions are exposed"* - Adam Gabbatt, May 28, 2018 via The Guardian

> *"Why the way we teach kids table manners is actually kind of racist"* - Joshna Maharaj, September 5, 2019 via Today's Parent

So far that's dogs, math, history, coffee shops, and good manners that are all racist. The list keeps going, as it always will because the outrage machine never sleeps. It's normal that as society progresses, the meaning or understanding of words evolves with that progression. The term retarded was used to replace mongoloid, which had fallen out of fashion. This in turn is being replaced as it is now considered offensive. Words or subjects will always face scrutiny and may no longer be considered acceptable in polite society. What's disturbing is the trend to categorize things that seem unimpeachable such as math or good manners, as racist. Yet here we are. There is even mild controversy surrounding the political correctness of the term black versus the term African American. I grew up in California, in the 1980s and was taught by just about everyone to use the term black and so that's the term I've used throughout this book and conversationally. However at least one person has told me they prefer African American, and I do my best to be respectful while they are a part of any conversation with me.

Should I cease to use that specific term entirely because that one person, or several people might find it offensive? It seems to be acceptable as it is used to promote social equity with the phrase black lives matter. Yet even if I were to cease to use the term black in reference to a group of people, this solution creates a dilemma for me. One of my friends has explained to me that African-American should be reserved for black people who actually come from an African country, and know the African culture from that part of the continent. These two differing perspectives on the subject present a challenge, but we're all respectful of one another's opinions, trust one another, and understand that none of us has ill intent. In 2016, Good Morning America, host Amy Robach ran afoul of the outrage machine when she used the phrase "colored people" instead of "people of color." She of course apologized because she likely just stumbled over her words. I doubt she had any ill intent when she spoke those words.

And it's that last piece that tips the scales for me. When evaluating another person's actions, I look at the context first, but more importantly I try to examine their intent. Intent is so important that it is integrated into our legal system. If someone dies because of my actions, is it murder? It might be but there are questions that need to be answered. Even if my actions constitute murder, did I commit 1st degree or 2nd degree murder? For that investigators would need to identify if my actions were premediated. Investigators might also ask did I intend for them to die? Perhaps I was simply negligent when I hit them with my car because I was sending a text message. Was I just in the wrong place at the wrong time? Maybe they jumped off an overpass and I just happened to be the car they landed on. There will be, and should be, a lot of questions to better understand the circumstances of the situation. While this is an extreme example, it illustrates the fact that context, and intent, matter when judging a situation.

The same analysis should apply even to something as benign or as offensive as the confederate flag. Evaluating the circumstances for the purchase is the only way to determine the intent of the buyer. For example, what if the person is buying a confederate flag as a part of a movie underscoring the racist past of the South and needs it as a prop? Pretty reasonable. What if they really like the television show, The Dukes of Hazzard. Daisy Duke played by Catherine Bach was a first celebrity crush for many young boys in the early 80's. A little weird, but no ill intentions by the buyer. What if a civil rights group goes to buy a confederate flag to burn[7] as a part of a demonstration in front of the Mississippi state capitol? A well-intentioned exercise of the first amendment. Afterall, American flags are often burned as a demonstration of free speech in protest of American policy, politics, or general existence. Even though I probably wouldn't be friends with a person determined to burn an American flag, I absolutely support their right to express themselves in this fashion.

A key difference here is that I refuse to act as the gatekeeper for what constitutes free speech, free thought, and free expression, and I certainly can't predict what your intent is when you go to make a purchase. Even with continually improving predictive analytics, Amazon hasn't achieved the ability to know what and why a purchase is

---

7

made. This is what makes Amazon's decision concerning. Amazon has made a statement that no person that purchases a confederate flag can ever have good intentions, and that statement is antithetical to a free society. Amazon has condemned a person before knowing their intent. Unless they're willing to admit it was actually just a publicity stunt designed to score social credit points.

That's about as strong a defense for the confederacy or confederate flags that I can muster. If you want my personal opinion on the confederate flag, I think it's the flag of a defeated army, and I'm probably not going to be friends with someone who waves it around dreaming of the rise of the South. I'm an American, and believe the United States is the best nation on the planet. I also understand that we, as a nation, aren't perfect, so I do my best to make things a little better each day. If I ever feel the need for a rebel flag, I'll choose the Moultrie flag. It's solid navy blue, with a white crescent in the upper left-hand corner inscribed with the word, Liberty. It was used during the American Revolution by a band of rebels seeking freedom from British tyranny. Now that I can get behind.

I get it though. Some people have the 'son of the South' identity, or they have some family link to the confederacy, or they just really like the Dukes of Hazzard and keep one of those flags around for nostalgia. Hate isn't necessarily in their heart, and I won't assume so before hearing what they have to say. On the other hand, if they're one of those people that's hanging on to dead ideologies and believe that the South shall rise again, and have a general support for segregation, get over it bud. The confederacy literally lost a war. Jump on board team America. We'd be glad to have someone so blindly loyal (160ish years really should be long enough to cope).

Again, I'm on team U.S.A. and feel extremely lucky to have been born here. I understand why so many people want to immigrate here and begrudge nobody who does so with good intentions (which I believe are most people, but not all). It's a huge risk to emigrate to another country legally, or otherwise. A person leaves their homelands, traveling hundreds or thousands of miles to a place where they probably don't speak the language, for the chance at a better life. It's not even a guarantee, it's a chance. It's a roll of the dice. I think that's a testament to the greatness of our country. I don't see a lot of people building rafts out of garbage trying to float down to Cuba for free medical school or hospital visits. That's what makes the rise of Amazon so spectacular. Amazon is the embodiment, and realization of the American dream. Even though some people may argue the merits of Amazon's success. Some people might point out that Amazon's corporate culture has been called demoralizing by some former employees. There have certainly been current and former Amazon employees that have come forward to complain about the harsh working conditions. Regardless of those flaws, it is tough to deny what Amazon has achieved. They are the pinnacle of what it means to build something great. It's because of their success that they're also able to provide charitable donations with programs like AmazonSmile.

AmazonSmile is a program that was launched in October 2013. It was designed as a way for Amazon to give back to the community. When a person opts in for AmazonSmile they can pick from an eligible 501(c)(3) organization and every time they make an eligible purchase, Amazon will donate 0.5% of the purchase price to the charity selected. While that doesn't sound like very much, Amazon performs so many transactions that even at 0.5% the small numbers start to add up. To date Amazon has donated over $200 million dollars to various charitable organizations across the globe. The program itself is administered by The AmazonSmile Foundation, a 501(c)(3) nonprofit created by Amazon. The operating costs for the AmazonSmile Foundation are paid for by Amazon. This means all of the money generated by the AmazonSmile program is donated to the charitable organizations selected by the program participants, and overall, it's a great program. I participate and choose to donate to Foster Angels On Earth, who I fully endorse. They work with adoption agencies to provide living necessities to foster children in need. The founder is probably the nicest person I've ever met.

Of course, there will always be detractors, and for some miserable people out there, Amazon will never be able to do enough. At least one of these miserable people pointed out they aren't willing to add a new bookmark to their browser so they can go to smile.amazon.com instead of amazon.com. Their reasoning: because 0.5% isn't worth it. To be fair they identified as marxists and having to do anything to earn money was a foreign concept to them. Ironically, they used the concept of the time-value of money while complaining. Again 0.5% isn't a lot, but it costs me no additional effort other than signing up and adding a new bookmark, and it's a nice way for me to support an organization I believe does good work for the community at large.

For the people who do see the value in providing donations to charitable causes AmazonSmile is an easy way to do so. But how does a person decide what charity to pick? That's a personal decision and there are literally over 1 million charities to choose from. Amazon doesn't choose what charity a person should direct their donations to, but they do make recommendations of qualified organizations. Those recommendations come from an eligible list of nonprofit organizations, and it's a list that Amazon also doesn't assemble. To decide what organizations are eligible for AmazonSmile, Amazon uses two groups. The first is the U.S. Office of Foreign Assets Control (OFAC). According to the description on their website, the OFAC:

> *"...administers and enforces economic and trade sanctions based on US foreign policy and national security goals against targeted foreign countries and regimes, terrorists, international narcotics traffickers, those engaged in activities related to the proliferation of weapons of mass destruction, and other threats to the national security, foreign policy or economy of the United States."*

That makes sense. Amazon operates in nearly every country on the planet, and there are charitable organizations across the globe. Making sure those organizations aren't funneling money to fund terrorist activities is a good thing and keeps Amazon from running afoul of any legal issues both in the U.S. and internationally.

The second group Amazon uses is the Southern Poverty Law Center or SPLC. The SPLC is a U.S. based group founded in 1971 by Morris Dees, Joseph J. Levin Jr., and Julian Bond. Originally intended to fight racial injustice in the democrat controlled south, the SPLC tackled issues such as poverty, racial discrimination, and the death penalty, and they've spent over four decades doing work to combat racism. Even with all the positive work the people there have done during that time, the SPLC has not escaped controversy. Over the years, complaints about how the SPLC classifies the hate group list they maintain have risen. The SPLC has been accused of weaponizing the list against groups with conservative politics primarily targeting conservative Christian groups whose religious beliefs prevent them from supporting marriage for same sex couples. They've also been accused of targeting conservative Christian groups who don't support abortion rights. There have also been reports of internal strife, and accusations of extravagant expenditures. The group's senior leaders have been accused of using funds to create what some employees term a 'Poverty Palace'. Accusations of spending abuses by nonprofit leadership is not uncommon. In 2016 the CEO and COO for Wounded Warrior Project were fired over a similar scandal.

However, the SPLC had even worse allegations come to light in early 2019 when an assistant legal director resigned alleging the organization had racial and gender equity problems. Dozens of SPLC employees co-signed a letter and sent it to the leadership team. In it they detailed allegations of unprofessional conduct, sexual harassment, discrimination, and most damning of all, racism. Some of the most egregious accusations were the reports that singled out SPLC leadership for engaging in behaviours that systematically harassed female, and minority employees. These accusations went all the way to the top. In response, the SPLC fired founder Morris Dees and removed his bio from their website. The SPLC gave a statement announcing they were going to hire an, *"...outside organization to conduct a comprehensive assessment of our internal climate and workplace practices."* In the fallout, SPLC President Richard Cohen, and Legal Director Rhonda Brownstein both resigned.

While these allegations do not negate the decades of positive work the SPLC has done, they do call into question the ability for them to remain a trusted, and neutral gatekeeper for a list of hate groups that is considered to be:

> *"authoritative and are widely accepted and cited in academic and media coverage of such groups and related issues"* - Wikipedia, September 18, 2020

If systemic racism, and discrimination exists with the organization, they certainly are in no position to determine who is and is not an extremist, and they certainly have no moral high ground when it comes to classifying hate groups. Beyond their own sins and internalized racism, it's concerning when SPLC states on its website that it:

> *"monitors and exposes the activities of the American radical right"* - SPLC, September 2020

It's concerning because the SPLC has no equivalent statement or policy regarding the radical left. At times, the SPLC even defends leftist terrorist groups. In one article published on their website, they go as far to say:

> *"There is an obvious ideological gulf separating the radical right, with its racist and fascist appeals, from the left-wing..."* - SPLC, May 8, 2001

The finish their statement by naming a terrorist group that has participated in bombings which I won't list here. The SPLC continues by defending the terror group by claiming they are advocates for, *"equality, social justice"* and they have a, *"compassion for all life"*. Why does any of this matter in a chapter about Amazon? Because Amazon, through the use of the SPLC as a gatekeeper has stopped people from donating to nonprofit groups such as the Alliance Defending Freedom (ADF), and the Pacific Justice Institute (PJI). These groups aren't fringe racist groups seeking the rise of segregation or espousing racist eugenic ideology. They're not even some fringe religious group spewing vile, hateful messages similar to groups like the one out of Topeka who used to picket funerals with horrific signs targeting everyone from the LBGT community to dead soldiers. Amazon actively disallows groups whose only sin is their sincerely held Christian beliefs. For example, the ADF was founded in 1993. Their mission is:

> *"advocating for religious liberty, the sanctity of human life, freedom of speech, and marriage and family"* - ADF, September 2020

They're a legal interest group that have successfully argued cases in the U.S. Supreme Court at least 9 separate occasions. The ADF also supports invocations at public meetings which have been argued against on grounds of the separation of church and state. The ADF supports the right for government bodies to pay for and maintain religious displays including crosses, nativity scenes, and Christmas decorations on public lands and in public buildings. The ADF also opposes abortion including the right for healthcare workers to refuse to participate in the performance of abortions, or any practices if those practices are contrary to the individual's moral principles. The ADF is opposed to same-sex marriage and civil unions and believes children should be raised by a married mother and father, and it's this last piece where they ran afoul of the SPLC.

In 2016 the SPLC added the ADF to their vaunted hate group list. The SPLC maintains a page that describes the ADF, a little of their history, and opens with a list of reasons that the SPLC uses to justify the hate group designation. I won't argue for or against SPLC's list here, but I did find something interesting about the ADF bio page the SPLC maintains. In a section titled, *In Its Own Words* is what a reader might expect, a list of quotes made by members of ADF that are used as evidence to support the SPLC hate allegations. Here is one such quote from the top of the list:

> *"Allowing males to compete in the female category isn't fair and destroys girls' athletic opportunities. Males will always have inherent physical advantages over comparably talented and trained girls—that's the reason we have girls' sports in the first place. And a male's belief about his gender doesn't eliminate those advantages."* – Christiana Holcomb, 2019 via SPLC

While this viewpoint may be disagreeable to some, I would hardly call it hate speech. It's clearly making an argument against a particular group of people, but certainly not in a hateful way. Maybe I'm being too literal. Let's take a look at what the FBI defines as a hate group.

> *"According to the United States Federal Bureau of Investigation (FBI), a hate group's primary purpose is to promote animosity, hostility, and malice against persons belonging to a race, religion, disability, sexual orientation, or ethnicity/national origin which differs from that of the members of the organization."* - Wikipedia, September 2020

Animosity is defined as strong hostility, and hostility is defined as hostile behaviour, unfriendliness, or opposition to, and admittedly Christiana Holcomb certainly appears in opposition to allowing transgender women compete in women's sports but I think people are allowed to be opposed to things they don't agree with or particularly like. I must admit I am hostile towards sweet pickles, but I certainly wouldn't consider myself hateful of people that make or eat them. I think that last piece, malice, is the differentiator here, and malice is defined as the intention or desire to do evil. Are Ms. Holcomb's intentions evil, does she wish to injure trans women? For context let's examine some of the other quotes SPLC lists for groups similarly listed as a hate group on their site.

"White Pride Worldwide" - Stormfront.org motto via SPLC

"God is the author of racism. God is the One who divided mankind into different types. ... Mixing the races is rebelliousness against God" - Council of Conservative Citizens website, 2001 via SPLC

"Every white man and every Jew is the devil by nature" - Hashim Nzinga, chairman, Sa Neter University, National Black Men's Convention, Washington DC, July 7, 2018 via SPLC

"Filthy sodomites crave legitimacy as dogs eating their own vomit & sows wallowing in their own feces crave unconditional love" - Westboro Baptist Church news release, Jan. 15, 1998 via SPLC

Is it really a comparison? Nothing about Ms. Holcomb's statement indicates hatred towards the trans community. In fact, none of the statements attributed to the ADF and provided by the SPLC website even come close to the horrific things many other groups make. While Ms. Holcomb certainly isn't supportive of the idea that a biological male should be allowed to compete in sports with a biological female; she doesn't dehumanize trans people. Her point is primarily focused around the biological differences when comparing XX and XY chromosome bearers. Those differences are very real, and that's why there are surgery options and hormonal treatments available to the trans community. So, what is the right answer? I don't know. I certainly don't share or support the ADF's core tenets about the LBGTQ community, nor do I share their beliefs about abortion. But I also don't share the SPLC's assertion that the ADF is a hate group, and I don't share the belief that ADF members hate women because they don't openly support abortion rights.

I also don't believe Dr. Ben Carson is an extremist that warrants listing on the SPLC website. But that's exactly what the SPLC did in October 2014. Dr. Carson is a retired neurosurgeon who is considered a pioneer in his field. He was a 2016 republican candidate for president and led nationwide polls for the republic nomination before the rise of President Trump. Dr. Carson is currently serving as the 17th United States Secretary of Housing and Urban Development. He's also an author, father, husband, and man of faith and has been a notable speaker at the National Prayer Breakfast on at least two occasions. According to Wikipedia, Dr. Carson has received, *"more than 60 honorary doctorate degrees and numerous national merit citations"*. He is the recipient of the Presidential Medal of Freedom, he was elected into the National Academy of Medicine, and in 2009 a TV movie about his life's work was made, starring Cuba Gooding Jr. So how did someone so distinguished make it onto the SPLC extremists list? According to the apology the SPLC issued in February 2015, *"Dr. Carson has, in fact, made a number of statements that express views that we believe most people would conclude are extreme."* Here's the extremist view they alleged:

> *"I think people have completely taken the*
> *wrong meaning out of what I was saying. First*
> *of all, I certainly believe gay people should*
> *have all the rights that anybody else has. What*
> *I was basically saying is that as far as*
> *marriage is concerned, that has traditionally*
> *been between a man and a woman, and*

nobody should be able to change that." - Dr. Ben Carson, March 29, 2013 via SPLC

While I disagree with Dr. Carson on this matter, I wouldn't call this an extreme view or even hateful. Disagreeable certainly, but even the SPLC admit that their listing, *"...did not meet our standards..."* to be considered extremist or hateful.

With these evaluations the SPLC is wading into dangerous territory. Especially when it begins conflating a lack of blind devotion, and support for liberal ideology with hate. While I wouldn't donate to the ADF, there are people who would, and I believe they have a right to despite the SPLC and their contentious label. For now, it seems the labels will stand. In 2019 a federal court ruled the SPLC had a first amendment right to label Florida based Christian organization, James Kennedy Ministries a hate group. The ministry group had initially sued both Amazon and the SPLC claiming it had been damaged by the hate-group label. In his opinion, Judge Mryon H. Thompson writes:

> *"If Coral Ridge disagrees with the 'hate group' designation, its hope for a remedy lies in the 'marketplace of ideas', not a defamation action."* - Judge Myron Thompson, 2019

Something else in Judge Thompson's ruling caught my eye. I think the judge makes an interesting point when he states:

> *"To find actual malice just because SPLC publicized a meaning of 'hate group' that conflicted with the common understanding of the term would severely undermine debate and free speech about a matter of public concern."* - Judge Myron Thompson, 2019

Judge Thompson precisely identifies the strategy that the SPLC has adopted whereby it leverages its position as a trusted institute to push a particular narrative that fits their brand of political beliefs. In doing so are using their unique position in the hopes of silencing conservative dissent. They are attempting to control information. It's not so much that the SPLC is redefining what the term hate group means, which is Judge Thompson's broader point about how societies evolve and progress over time. Rather the concern is that they are intentionally using that new definition in a misleading, and insidious manner. The SPLC has weaponized their hatewatch list to label opposing political ideologies. They are using that power and the power of association to create a narrative in the public's mind that aligns sincerely held religious beliefs with the grotesque nature of extreme racism and bigotry.

And Amazon is enabling them. By allowing SPLC to control the conversation and silence a conservative voice, Amazon is denying equitable service to a segment of their customer base because of their religious beliefs, and the public is beginning to take notice. On August 24, 2020 Congressman Doug Collins provided a press release where he and 14 other Republicans provided an open letter written to Amazon CEO Jeff Bezos regarding how Amazon utilizes information from the SPLC. Specifically, they state:

> *"Amazon relies in part on information from the Southern Poverty Law Center (SPLC) to exclude certain non-profits from participating in Amazon's charity-support program, AmazonSmile. [Bezos] also acknowledged that Amazon's approach is imperfect, and said you welcome suggestions for improvement. Given SPLC's bias against certain conservative non-profits, we write to learn more about Amazon's reliance on and empowerment of the SPLC."*

The Bezos acknowledgement they refer to is the congressional testimony provided by Bezos in July 2020. During his time Congressman Matt Gaetz questioned why religious organizations such as the Catholic Family News, the American Family Association, and the Jewish Defense

League were being excluded from participating in the AmazonSmile program.

> ***Gaetz:*** *I'm just wondering why you would place your confidence in a group that seems to be so out of step and seems to take mainstream Christian doctrine and label it as hate?*

> ***Bezos:*** *We use the Southern Poverty Law Center data to say which charities are extremist organizations, we also use the U.S. Foreign Asset Office to do the same thing, those two together...*

> ***Gaetz:*** *But why? Since they're calling Catholics and these Jewish groups hateful groups, why would you trust them?*

> ***Bezos:*** *Sir, I'm going to acknowledge this is an imperfect system and...*

> ***Gaetz:*** *No doubt.*

> ***Bezos:*** *And I would like suggestions on better or additional sources for how to...*

> ***Gaetz:*** *My suggestion would be a divorce from the SPLC.*

Congressman Gaetz goes on to observe that at one point the SPLC considered Dr. Ben Carson an extremist (though Gaetz did confuse the extremist label SPLC issued with being listed as an extremist group). It's not just Congressman Gaetz who's fed up with SPLC's behaviour. The Coalition for Jewish Values is also calling for Amazon to end its partnership with the SPLC. In an open letter signed by more than 100 Jewish rabbinic leaders across the U.S. point out that, *"...the SPLC 'hate map' is uniquely detrimental and even dangerous to the Jewish community…"*. In the letter they cite the SPLC's open hostility towards groups with sincerely held religious beliefs, stating:

> *"While the SPLC is careful not to denigrate the Bible or other religious texts directly, it frequently vilifies groups based upon nothing more than their advocacy for biblically based beliefs about sexual and family ethics that were uncontroversial a generation or two ago."*

The letter continues by questioning SPLC's motives. The rabbis point out that the hate group list leaves out groups that are directly tied to international terrorist organizations, and groups expressing anti-Semitic beliefs. The rabbis also call out the SPCL's hypocrisy when they identify SPLC's partnership with the Council on American-Islamic Relations. During trial and under oath an FBI Special Agent testified that CAIR is nothing more than a front for Hamas. Hamas is a designated terrorist organization according to the United States, the European Union, and Israel. The letter also points out that SPLC was forced to pay $3.38 million dollars, and issue public apologies after the SPLC defamed Maajid Nawaz, a Muslim man, and several others when they had labeled them anti-Muslim extremists. The rabbis end the letter by imploring Jeff Bezos:

> *"On behalf of the Jewish community and all who share concern for our lives and safety, we urge you to immediately terminate any association between Amazon Smile and the SPLC"*

Shareholders are also beginning to take notice. In an article published by FoxBusiness and written by James Langford, note that conservative investor Justin Danhof submitted a proposal that was voted on during Amazon's annual meeting. In it, Danhof requests that Amazon:

> *"examine whether a company charity's use of
> the Southern Poverty Law Center as a
> gatekeeper in selecting recipients has led to
> discrimination against right-leaning
> organizations"* - Justin Danhof, May 27, 2020
> via FoxBusiness

It was one of 12 resolutions considered at the meeting and he was able to raise the proposal thanks in part to The Free Enterprise Project. They are an advocacy group that uses rules allowing people who own a sufficient amount of stock to introduce proposals at these types of annual meetings. Mr. Danhof echoed the sentiments of both the rabbis, and the U.S. congressmen:

> *"the SPLC is a widely discredited, very
> partisan organization that uses its hate map to
> try to put Christian conservative organizations
> on a par with the Ku Klux Klan. Amazon is
> basically in a very weird extreme here. It's
> admittedly engaging in viewpoint
> discrimination in its charitable program. We
> called them out on it, and they endorsed it."*
> Justin Danhof, May 27, 2020 via FoxBusiness

Ultimately Amazon's attempts to silence conservative and religious voices may not matter much. While it's clear Amazon is engaging proxies such as the SPLC to execute their viewpoint discrimination as Mr. Danhof puts it. The impact of this bias is felt over too broad of an area. It would be like giving away $100 million dollars to combat poverty, but only giving $1 to 100 million different people. While it would certainly be nice to get a free dollar, there would be no measurable improvement for outcomes for those who are suffering. Still it's one more channel where the liberal narratives are the driving force behind attempts to silence conservative dissent. Even though Mr. Danhof's actions may seem like a mild political stunt, they may be the leading edge on a wave of pushback building against companies who are actively engaged in disinformation campaigns.

chapter 9: life in the time of collusion

I had to write a chapter about covid-19 and the blatant manipulation of information spread by various actors and groups. It will focus on the U.S., and because I live in Philadelphia it will have a slant towards policies enacted both in the city, and the state as a whole. I think from the very beginning the entire world was lied to about what the best things to do were, and the amount of contradicting information that came out during the first few weeks of the crisis undermined people's willingness to believe anything. The response from government bodies, the liberal media, and digital tech companies all contributed to the confusion and frustration that created two loose camps of people. One camp thought it was all a hoax and or an overreaction and went around licking toilet seats to prove it. The other camp showered in alcohol and gasoline, wore chemical suits, and wouldn't answer calls because they might covid-19 through the phone. Okay maybe not that bad, but the way the media covered the story you would think it was true.

Most people were on board for the first two weeks the country shut down. I think most people begrudgingly agreed to the next two weeks. After that frustration started to build, and many people were over it. Most of the small business owners I knew at the time just wanted to get back to work. But there were people who genuinely didn't want to work and just used covid-19 as a cover for staying home. There were people genuinely scared of covid-19, and there were people who didn't give a fuck. Sadly, there were people who lost their lives. I think by the end most people just went along with the masks and the shutdowns because it was easier than fighting the entire world. Regardless of what camp you were in it was a strange time to be alive, and the flow of information became more important than ever. So, watching Google, YouTube, Twitter, Facebook, and all the corporate media channels collude to keep the public following a single, liberal narrative was bizarre and the most frightening thing I've experienced in my life.

Congress shall make no law respecting an establishment of religion, or prohibiting the free exercise thereof; or abridging the freedom of speech, or of the press; or the right of the people peaceably to assemble, and to petition the Government for a redress of grievances.

2020 is the year of the rat according to the Chinese Zodiac. Apparently, that rat brought the plague with it. Severe acute respiratory syndrome coronavirus 2 (SARS-CoV-2); more commonly known as covid-19, coronavirus, or if we're being more familiar, the 'rona. A pandemic. Or was it? It's just the flu. It's real. It's from a bat. It's from China. It's from a lab. It's from 5G towers. Implement travel restrictions. Travel restrictions are racist, come down to Chinatown. We should have had travel bans sooner. Call it Wuhan virus. Call it corona. Call it China virus. That's racist call it covid-19. Half of Italy is dead. It's not that bad. 50 million people are projected to die. No Bill Gates predicted 33 million. No, it's going to be 3 million. Nurses are dying from exhaustion! Look at those nurses on tik tok. It's only killing old people. Boomer remover! That's ageist. Masks don't work. Don't wear a mask. Wear a mask. Believe the doctors, wait not those doctors. Never has the discovery of a new virus been more divisive, nor its existence polarizing as is the case with covid-19. The one thing that everyone agreed on for this emergency: buy all the toilet paper.

On December 31, 2019, there were reports coming out of Hubei Province. They identified a cluster of deadly pneumonia-like cases in the city of Wuhan. News of this outbreak began to spread, and by January 6, 2020 the U.S. realized it could help. Director of the CDC Dr. Robert Redfield offered to send a team of scientists to assist China in containing the outbreak and collect information about this new virus. The Chinese Communist Party refused the offer. As it turns out it, the CCP refused international help because they were actively hiding, destroying, and falsifying evidence and information from the rest of the world. There is almost no reliable information available from Wuhan or from the early days of the outbreak because of this. The world will never have a clear picture of what happened in Wuhan, and the decision by the CCP to ignore offers of help delayed the global response covid-19. The Chinese Communist Party cost countless lives.

It took until January 7, 2020 for Chinese health officials to confirm the Wuhan cluster was caused by a coronavirus. With some information finally available, the CDC was able to issue an official health advisory and begin efforts in coordinating U.S. containment efforts with the rest of the world. Key to those efforts was knowing if human-to-human transmission was possible. Knowing the answer to this question would establish the foundation for how to effectively combat the spread of the disease. However, the Chinese Communist Party intentionally deceived the world when it stated there was no clear evidence that human-to-human transmission was possible. This deception likely costs tens of thousands of lives as it delayed an effective response in containing the deadly disease. Even worse, the World Health Organization (WHO) issued this statement:

> *"Preliminary investigations conducted by the Chinese authorities have found no clear evidence of human-to-human transmission of the novel #coronavirus (2019-nCoV) identified in #Wuhan, #China"* - WHO, January 14, 2020

The experts the world placed their trust in were actively disseminating what turned out to be communist propaganda. But at the time, the world still trusted the WHO and the CDC issued an update on January 17, 2020 stating that human-to-human transmission remained unconfirmed. Three days later with the eyes of the world turned to them, the Chinese Communist Party finally admitted that human-to-human transmission was detected which they had likely known since mid-December. Up to this point, the CCP was insistent there was no crisis, and so the world believed them.

Sixteen days later, on January 30, 2020, faced with overwhelming evidence, the WHO was finally forced to declare covid-19 a public health emergency. The WHO issued its highest-level warning, stating that, *"all countries should be prepared for containment"*. Director General of the WHO, Dr Tedros Adhanom Ghebreyesus claimed they declared this emergency because of the danger coronavirus presented to the world. It was a stunning that both China, and the WHO failed to act sooner, and it had deadly consequences. China's refusal to allow health experts access to Wuhan had delayed the global response in containment, and potential treatment. In what appears to be a coordinated effort to cover up for the Chinese Communist Party, Dr. Ghebreyesus deflected questions regarding the CCP. He refused to acknowledge the CCP failure to cooperate and disclose vital information to the rest of the world. During a press conference held by the WHO, Dr. Ghebreyesus claims:

> *"China is to be congratulated for the extraordinary measures it has taken to contain the outbreak despite the severe social and economic impact that it is having on China."* - Tedros Adhanom Ghebreyesus, January 30, 2020 via WHO.int

He goes on to state that, *"...we must act together now to limit further spread,"* which makes sense. However, he follows that up by claiming, *"there is no reason for measures that unnecessarily interfere with international travel and trade."* These appear to be contradictory statements designed to protect the Chinese economy due to their reliance on manufacturing exports.

Why would the WHO and Dr. Ghebreyesus focus on protecting the Chinese Communist Party? Perhaps it would help to know that Dr. Ghebreyesus is an Ethiopian national, and previously held two ministry positions in the Ethiopian government. Ethiopia is a small, east African nation with a GDP of approximately $100 billion (USD). China represents 60% of all foreign investment into

Ethiopia. What is China buying in Ethiopia? Likely it's political favors. China invested $475 million (USD) for a railway system in the Ethiopian capital as a joint venture. Chinese investors also provided $2.4 billion (USD) in funding for the Addis Ababa–Djibouti Railway. This is a critical piece of infrastructure that provides a link from Ethiopia's capital city to portage in Djibouti. As minister of foreign affairs for Ethiopia from 2012 through 2016, Dr. Ghebreyesus would have had direct dealings with any foreign institutes investing in such a large scale and important project. Primary construction of the rail line began in 2011 and ran through 2016, and it was inaugurated in Ethiopia on October 5 of that year.

This isn't some fringe conspiracy theory. U.S. Secretary of State Michael Pompeo stated in July 2020 that the U.S. has intelligence that shows China used their influence to get Dr. Ghebreyesus installed as WHO director. Likely an effort to leverage his role there. Even the Atlantic admits China is buying influence across the globe. They published an article titled, *China's Bargain on Global Influence Is Paying Off.* In the article, Rear Admiral Kenneth Bernard, a former biodefense, and political advisor is quoted as saying:

> *"[China] give as little money as will buy influence"* - Rear Admiral Kenneth Bernard,
> May 6, 2020 via the Atlantic

From Dr. Ghebreyesus' statements during the covid-19 crisis, that strategy appears to be paying off. Despite the disinformation campaign peddled by the Chinese Communist Party, by January 31, 2020 the U.S. finally had enough information to be able to declare a public health emergency. That same day President Trump signed the travel restriction orders related to covid-19. From the U.S. State Department website:

> *On Friday, January 31, President Trump signed a proclamation suspending entry into the United States of aliens who were physically*

*present in the People's Republic of China,
excluding the Special Administrative Regions of
Hong Kong and Macau, within the 14 days
preceding entry or attempted entry into the
United States. The proclamation took effect
Sunday, February 2. This action followed the
declaration of a public health emergency in the
United States related to the novel coronavirus
outbreak in Wuhan, China.*

It was a temporary measure designed to directly address
the early stages of the pandemic the world found itself in.
How did the U.S. respond to President Trump's actions?
Liberals, and the Chinese Communist Party were critical of
the move, and various sources commented on the travel
restrictions:

*"...unceasingly manufactured and spread
panic..."* - Hua Chunying, Chinese Communist
Party diplomat, February 3, 2020

*"How Trump's Panicky Coronavirus Travel Ban
Cost Me $4,000 in 2 Hours to Save My Job"* -
Sissi Cao, reporter, February 3, 2020 via the
Observer

*"The Trump administration's quarantine and
travel ban in response to the Wuhan
coronavirus could undercut international efforts
to fight the outbreak"* - Alice Miranda Ollstein,
reporter, February 4, 2020 via Politico

"...probably doesn't make sense..." - Ami Bera,
U.S. Representative (D), February 4, 2020

*"...an overreaction that causes unnecessary
fear and weakens the global response..."* - Sam
Levin, reporter, February 4, 2020 via the
Guardian

Even democratic candidate Joe Biden chimed in and called President Trump's travel ban xenophobic. In an article published by CNN, Jake Tapper writes:

> *"Biden first accused Trump of xenophobia in dealing with the coronavirus pandemic on January 31, at a campaign rally in Fort Madison, Iowa"* - Jake Tapper, April 3, 2020 via CNN

Yet just 2 months later the Biden campaign claims he supported the travel restrictions. In the same CNN article, Kate Bedingfeld, one of Joe Biden's campaign managers is quoted as stating:

> *"Joe Biden supports travel bans that are guided by medical experts, advocated by public health officials, and backed by a full strategy"* - Kate Bedingfeld, April 3, 2020 via CNN

In speaking directly about President Trump's travel restriction Kate says, *"Science supported this ban, therefore he did too"*. It represented a complete manipulation of the narrative surrounding the U.S. approach to mitigating the impact of covid-19. Not an uncommon strategy used by all politicians but foreshadowed the way information would be manipulated throughout the crisis.

Through the remainder of February and into March, travel restrictions and recommendations continued to roll out. On March 19, 2020, the U.S. State Department issued a blanket advisory that U.S. citizens should try and avoid international travel completely. March also saw something new implemented across the nation: lockdowns. Government mandated lockdowns were being implemented and enforced at the state level. For Pennsylvania, the order was given by then ~~democratic Governor~~ Dear Leader Tom Wolf on March 16, 2020. Similar orders were issued across the country. At the time it was believed these orders would save lives. Only 7 states never issued lockdown orders:

Utah, Wyoming, North Dakota, South Dakota, Nebraska, Iowa, and Arkansas. The remaining 43 states shut down their economies, directed their citizens to stay home, and restricted travel. It was the most widespread abuse of authority ever executed in the United States, violating the rights of more than 300 million citizens. Most people just went along silently nodding.

The political ramifications of the lockdown have yet to be tallied, as does the impact to small business. So far, the outcomes look bleak. As of September 2020, voters seem prepared to dump the fall out of the shutdowns in the laps of democrats. Time will tell. There are several developed nations that never implemented lockdown's that appear to have outperformed the rest of the globe in mortality rates. We'll never know if the lockdowns had any positive effect on reducing the impact of covid-19.

Part of the reason we'll never know is the glaring misinformation campaigns executed by the Chinese Communist Party. Another reason is that the American Public was being lied to by the very people we were expected to trust. As early as February 2020, people in the U.S. were being actively discouraged from wearing masks by medical professionals. In an article from the Moffitt Cancer Center they state:

> *"Face masks are typically used by health professionals during surgery to shield them from exposure to bacteria encased in liquid droplets. While these masks have been found to reduce the chance of getting the flu by nearly 70%, they do not protect against airborne particles, which can easily find a way through the crevices. Although these face masks are available for anyone to purchase, there has been no sufficient evidence that would recommend the wearing of one. In fact, some experts suggest that there is potential harm that may come with wearing them. If you are around an infectious virus and touch the front of the mask at any point, there is the risk of*

contaminating yourself if you touch your face throughout the day, adjust your mask or even when you take it off.

Moffitt Cancer Center infectious disease expert Dr. John Greene says that unless you reside in Wuhan, wearing a face mask may be a bit of overkill and offer a false sense of security." - Moffitt Cancer Center, February 5, 2020

Moffitt Cancer Center weren't the only healthcare professionals pushing this narrative. The U.S. Surgeon General issued the same advice in a tweet:

"Seriously people - STOP BUYING MASKS!

They are NOT effective in preventing general public from catching #Coronavirus, but if healthcare providers can't get them to care for sick patients, it puts them and our communities at risk!" - @Surgeon_General, Vice Admiral Jerome Adams, February 29, 2020

In fact, the very masks U.S. citizens were instructed not to wear make the same claim. In a post that went viral in June 2020, an image showing the warning label on the side of a box of masks was shared. That warning stated:

"This product is an ear loop mask. This product is not a respirator and will not provide any protection against covid-19 (coronavirus) or other viruses or contaminants."

While that's true, masks are in fact shown to be a valuable tool at slowing the spread of microbial contaminants carried by water droplets. That's why on April 4, 2020 the CDC revised their policy and began advising the public to wear face masks covering the nose and mouth. In the policy recommendation the CDC asks the public not to purchase critical surgical masks or N95 masks that were needed for healthcare workers but instead to make reusable cloth masks. What did the WHO have to say about masks? At the time, their guidelines still advised against healthy individuals wearing masks. An article published CNBC on April 2, 2020 confirms this. The writer Sam Merideth discusses the U.S. policy on masks and states that the WHO website still advises:

> *"if you are healthy, you only need to wear a mask if you are taking care of a person with suspected 2019-nCoV infection"* - WHO, April 2020 via CNBC

The article also notes that the United Nations had said that masks were:

> *"effective only when used in combination with frequent hand-cleaning with alcohol-based hand rub or soap and water"* - Sam Merideth, April 2, 2020 via CNBC

In fact, as late as May 29, 2020 the CDC and the WHO mask wearing guidelines remained in opposition. In an article published by ABC News, Erin Schumaker notes the difference in recommendations when they write:

> *"The World Health Organization's guidance about when to wear a face mask may seem confusing to Americans, who have been advised by the Centers for Disease Control and Prevention to wear cloth face masks in public to help slow the spread of covid-19"* - Erin Schumaker, May 29, 2020 via ABC News

Why the mixed messaging between public health officials, and why did the CDC revise their guidance? If healthcare professionals already knew masks were effective at reducing the transmission of other human-to-human viruses such as influenza, why not err on the side of caution? Governmental agencies do that quite often. For example, milk is generally safe past its printed expiration date for a few reasons. The first being all commercial dairy products in the U.S. are pasteurized reducing the chances for microbial contamination. The second reason is when determining expiration dates the FDA takes a conservative approach. They advise producers to take a similar caution when printing expiration dates. This is by design and is intended to protect the public against harmful food poisoning. If covid-19 was projected to kill millions of people, why wouldn't that same cautionary approach be taken?

Perhaps Dr. Fauci can explain. During an interview with The Street host, Katherine Ross, Dr. Fauci responds to the question of why the public wasn't advised to wear masks from the beginning of the crisis:

> *"Well, the reason for that is that we were concerned, the public health community, and many people were saying this, were concerned that it was at a time when personal protective equipment, including the N95 masks and the surgical masks, were in very short supply. And we wanted to make sure that the people namely, the health care workers, who were brave enough to put themselves in harms way, to take care of people who you know were infected with the coronavirus and the danger of them getting infected"* - Dr. Anthony Fauci, June 12, 2020

That's a nice sentiment, but it's also extremely deceptive and erodes public trust. The recommendation that advised against wearing masks wasn't based on science, it was based entirely on fear. U.S. citizens were told an outright lie to protect a certain class of people. Even though this outright lie may have been a noble goal and an effort that should have been supported by the broader community, it was pure manipulation. Further, even when the CDC recommendations were revised, they specifically stated that the public could use cloth masks to mitigate the spread of covid-19. The recommendation to use cloth masks could have been made much sooner. However, in the early days people were shamed into not buying or wearing masks because the public was specifically told they didn't need them. This lie was promulgated by major news media outlets as demonstrated earlier, and by all digital tech companies. An article published by Vox notes that:

> *"Social media companies are increasing their vigilance about removing coronavirus conspiracies. Facebook, in particular, continues to update its policies as the outbreak, and corresponding disinformation spreads"* - Shirin Ghaffary & Rebecca Heilweil, March 4, 2020 via Vox

The digital tech world was complicit in this disinformation campaign. These companies directly pushed the CDC and WHO narratives and actively suppressed information that disputed what is now known to be unscientific guidance. This is not a baseless accusation. These companies proudly boast to doing so, in the same article the writers note that:

> *"Facebook, Twitter, YouTube, and TikTok have all told Recode that they've been working to promote factual content and some are limiting the reach of posts with misinformation on their platforms. Twitter, for instance, has put a warning label linking to the Centers for Disease Control and Prevention (CDC) when users search "coronavirus." Meanwhile, the WHO has now joined TikTok in an effort to boost accurate information about the illness, and several of those companies met with the public health organization at Facebook back in February."* - Shirin Ghaffary & Rebecca Heilweil, March 4, 2020 via Vox

Going one step further Facebook reportedly told Recode that they would:

"remove false claims and conspiracy theories flagged by world health organizations" - Shirin Ghaffary & Rebecca Heilweil, March 4, 2020 via Vox

While many of the false claims and conspiracy theories were correctly debunked, such as the claim 5G towers were spreading the virus, not everything was a fringe conspiracy. The no mask campaign perpetrated by the CDC and WHO are prime examples of this. It's not so much that these companies were blocking outrageous claims, it's that they weren't allowing any dissent from the narrative and it's this dangerous control of information that is startling.

Most people have never heard of John Yudkin. He was the British scientist that warned, or tried to warn, the world that heavy consumption of sugar is a severe health risk. For decades everyone knew fat was bad for you. All the science said so of course. Yet in 1972 John Yudkin published a book titled, *Pure, White and Deadly,* that condemned sugar as a deadly food additive. Yudkin was widely ridiculed. The commercial food industry, and other established academic minds set out to destroy Yudkin's reputation, some going as far as calling his work science fiction. These attacks had the desired effect as obesity rates have continued to rise for decades. Decades later University of California San Francisco professor of endocrinology Robert Lustig calls Yudkin's research groundbreaking. Lustig goes further and compares sugar to alcohol, tobacco, and even cocaine due to its negative effects on the human body. Humanity lost decades of time to combat the rise of obesity. While the deleterious effects of sugar on a person's health may seem like common knowledge now, in Yudkin's time it was wrongthink. The gatekeepers for information in 1972 wouldn't allow dissenting views, and so Yudkin was punished severely for it. Facebook, Twitter, Google, and YouTube are waging a similar war of censorship and control today. Each of these digital technology companies is using their power to silence dissent; harkening back to the days when fervent mobs would shout, "burn the heretic!"

5G cellular towers are not likely to be uncovered as the culprit behind the spread of covid-19, and nobody should drink bleach. Its chilling how easy it was for nearly all media outlets and digital tech companies to silence voices of dissent because it wasn't just fringe conspiracy theories these companies were silencing. There were real doctors, and real science being attacked. Enter the most politically debated drug ever hydroxychloroquine. On March 17, 2020 a French doctor, and microbiologist Didier Raoult made a stunning announcement. Quick bio, Dr. Raoult earned his bachelor's degree in literature before being admitted to medical school in Marseille, France where he specialized in infectious diseases. Continuing, Dr. Raoult announced that during a small trial involving 24 patients the use of azithromycin and hydroxychloroquine appeared to be an effective treatment for covid-19. Three days later Dr. Raoult published his preliminary findings with the International Journal of Antimicrobial Agents. While not conclusive, and far from comprehensive it was a potential lead, and with the world looking for answers, it was a place to start.

The news generated excitement, and Olivier Veran, the French Health Minister recommended additional testing to determine if Dr. Raoult's findings were repeatable. If the results were able to be replicated for a larger group of patients it would be a game changer. It would have meant the largest international industrial ramp effort in the history of mankind to make enough medication to supply the world. This would be an enormous decision, so before making such a huge investment in resources, all vested parties wanted to ensure the results were reliable. It would be irresponsible to tout this as the solution unless absolutely true.

However, on March 17, 2020 a wrinkle occurred. Trump spoke positively about the drug Dr. Raoult had used in his study, and the orange man bad gang spun into action. I'm going to give a lengthy quote here to demonstrate the exact words, phrasing, and in context statements President Trump made that day.

"If treatments known to be safe in Europe, Japan, or other nations are effective against the virus, we'll use that information to protect the health and safety of American people. Nothing will stand in our way as we pursue any avenue to find what best works against this horrible virus.

Now, a drug called chloroquine - and some people would add to it hydroxy. Hydroxychloroquine. So chloroquine or hydroxychloroquine. Now, this is a common malaria drug. It is also a drug used for strong arthritis. If somebody has pretty serious arthritis, also uses this in a somewhat different form. But it is known as a malaria drug, and it's been around for a long time and it's very powerful.

But the nice part is, it's been around for a long time, so we know that if it, if things don't go as planned, it's not going to kill anybody. When you go with a brand-new drug, you don't know that that's going to happen. You have to see and you have to go - long test. But this has been used in different forms, very powerful drug, in different forms. And it's shown very encouraging - very, very encouraging early results.

And we're going to be able to make that drug available almost immediately. And that's where the FDA has been so great. They, they've gone through the approval process. It's been approved. And they did it. They took it down from many, many months to immediate. So we're going to be able to make that drug available by prescription or states.

I spoke with Governor Cuomo about it at great length last night, and he wants to be right on, on the, he wants to be first on line. And so I think that's a tremendous, there's tremendous promise, based on the results and other tests. There's tremendous promise.

And normally the FDA would take a long time to approve something like that, and it's - it was approved very, very quickly and it's now approved, by prescription. Individual states will handle it. They can handle it. Doctors will handle it. And I think it's going to be, I think it's going to be great. Then we're quickly studying this drug, and while we're continuing to study it, but the studying is going to be also done in, as it's given out to large groups of people, perhaps in New York and other places. We'll study it there.

There are promising therapies produced by Gilead, and that's remdesivir. Remdesivir. And that's a drug used for other purposes that's been out and has had very good results for other purposes, but it seems to have a very good result, having to do with this virus. And that drug also has been approved or very close to approved, in that case, by the FDA.

And I can't tell you how much we appreciate what the FDA - these people are incredible patriots. And the job that Stephen Hahn is doing, Dr. Hahn, who is one of the most respected doctors in the country, by the way, where we took him. I said, "You sure you want to do this?" Now, we didn't know that this was going to be in the playlist, what happened here, but he really has stepped up to the plate, wherever you are. Where is he? You really have.

"Thank you, sir" - Stephen Hahn M.D.

I'd shake his hand, but I'm not supposed to do that. I'd get in a lot of trouble if I did that. But he's been fantastic. And I thank you, Doctor. He's going to speak right after I'm finished. So, Regeneron, again, and, is some, is a company that's done fantastically well, as I understand, with Ebola and some other things. Great company. And they're looking at some very promising events also. So you have remdesivir and you have chloroquine, and hydro, hydroxychloroquine. So those are two that are out now, essentially approved for prescribed use.

And I think it's going to be very exciting. I think it could be a game changer and maybe not. And maybe not. But I think it could be, based on what I see, it could be a game changer. Very powerful. They're very powerful.

So I want every American to know that we're doing everything we can. And these actions are important next steps. I mean, for the FDA to act the way they acted, with this kind of speed, is an incredible thing. Normally, they would say, "Well, we could have it by next year" or "We could have it by, in two years from now." You understand. This is the way, normally, it's like years and years and years. They had it immediately, based on the fact that it's been used for other things, totally unrelated things.

We believe these therapeutics and others under evaluation right now will be able to provide relief to many Americans. We really hope that's going to be. This could be a tremendous breakthrough. Tremendous breakthrough. And we will work toward a much-needed vaccine in the future, as I said. And what we're doing with the FDA is so exciting in so many other fields. So many things are happening. It's a very exciting time for, for medicine."

The full comments by President Trump lasted approximately 15 minutes, and this section reflects the full, in context, unedited comments he made regarding hydroxychloroquine. President Trump literally states that there are very early, encouraging results, referring to the report released by Dr. Raoult. In fact, he states there are promising results twice, and quite frankly at that point in time, these results showed promise.

Immediately headlines across almost every news outlet began reading that President Trump was endorsing an unapproved medication, and the orange man bad gang piled it on. Pharmacies began running out, but the medication is not purchasable by an individual without a prescription from a doctor. News outlets were quick to lay this at President Trump's feet. CNN, Bloomberg, NBC all ran with headlines distorting President Trump's statements.

"Fact check: Trump wrongly claims FDA 'approved' drug chloroquine to treat the coronavirus" - CNN, March 19, 2020

"'Lifesaving' lupus drug in short supply after Trump touts possible coronavirus treatment" - NBC, March 23, 2020

"Trump Touts Drug That FDA Says Isn't Yet Approved for Virus" - Bloomberg, March 19, 2020

Then on March 23, 2020 the attacks escalated. Two people were hospitalized, and one of them died, when the married couple ingested a lethal dose of chloroquine phosphate. Chloroquine phosphate used in fish tank cleaner, and is a completely different chemical compound than chloroquine, or hydroxychloroquine. That didn't matter. NBC News Correspondent Heidi Przybyla sent out a series of tweets that day condemning President Trump for what liberals began describing as reckless actions. In her tweets Heidi quoted the individual that survived as saying:

> *"Oh my God. Don't take anything. Don't believe anything. Don't believe anything that the President says and his people because they don't know what they're talking about. And don't take anything--be so careful and call your doctor. This is a heart ache I'll never get over." -* Wanda Lenius via @HeidiNBC, Heidi Przybyla, March 23, 2020

It was all the orange man bad gang needed. The news cycle was filled with outrageous claims that President Trump had killed the man who died. On March 27, 2020 Stat News posted one of the only sensible articles at the time, *What if hydroxychloroquine doesn't work? What if it does? Right now, we don't know.* In the article, writer Matthew Herper correctly states:

> *"This week [hydroxychloroquine] made headlines, due in part to tweets from President Trump and in part because of a small French study of 42 patients that seemed to show that hydroxychloroquine, particularly when combined with the antibiotic azithromycin, helped decrease patients' levels of coronavirus. Unfortunately, the rumors about the drug's efficacy have also encouraged some to buy and even consume a similarly named fish tank cleaner; one person has died.*
>
> *But a second study emerged last week from Shanghai University in China of 30 patients*

hospitalized for Covid-19. Whether patients received hydroxychloroquine or not, their body temperature returned to normal a day after hospitalization, and the time it took for levels of the virus to become undetectable was comparable. Unlike the study from France, the patients in this study were randomly assigned to either hydroxychloroquine or the control group, which makes the results more reliable."

Harper goes on to cite Zach Weinberg of Flatiron Health. Weinberg is quoted as saying:

"Sometimes people confuse saying, 'the study doesn't tell you anything' with saying the drug doesn't work. That's a really important distinction. They're not the same thing. I'm not saying the drug doesn't work or does work. What I'm actually saying is nobody knows if the drug works or doesn't work."

We didn't know at the time if hydroxychloroquine would work as a treatment or prophylaxis for covid-19. And that is what early, promising, and encouraging results mean. They had potential. We don't know, and we didn't know how hydroxychloroquine would work in treating covid-19. Both studies Harper cites in their article were early results with limited data. There was limited certainty into the efficacy of hydroxychloroquine at that time, and President Trump was correct when he said the results were early, and he was correct when he stated there were going to be testing it in studies in New York, which was the hardest hit region at the time. President Trump was also correct when he stated that hydroxychloroquine was already approved by the FDA. Hydroxychloroquine is approved by the FDA for general use by a prescribing doctor if the doctor feels it would be an effective treatment for their patient. So, if all the things President Trump had said were true, why would news media outlets publish stories with such misleading headlines? Say the line: orange man bad!

On April 1, 2020 a doctor named Peter Hotez gave an interview to Joe Rogan. For reference Dr. Hotez is a:

> *"pediatrician, and advocate in the fields of global health, vaccinology, and neglected tropical disease control. He serves as founding dean of the National School of Tropical Medicine and Professor of Pediatrics and Molecular Virology & Microbiology at Baylor College of Medicine, where he is also Director of the Texas Children's Hospital Center for Vaccine Development and Texas Children's Hospital Endowed Chair in Tropical Pediatrics."*
> - Wikipedia, September 2020

During the interview one of the subjects that came up was hydroxychloroquine. Dr. Hotez gives a great description on the history of the drug and what it's been used for and I highly recommend listening to the Joe Rogan podcast for Hotez's more complete explanation. But specifically, for covid-19, Dr. Hotez had this to say:

> *"We were there about a decade ago with influenza that this hydroxychloroquine also inhibited the influenza virus in the test tube. But then it didn't pan out in larger clinical studies. So I think we have to be really careful and don't be too quick to say, Okay, this is going to be it. We're not even close to that yet, but we'll know in the next few weeks because we're working hard to scale up clinical trials looking at that medicine."* - Dr. Hotez, April 1, 2020

Here we have a literal expert on the treatment of diseases saying hydroxychloroquine has potential, but that we need to scale up clinical trials, echoing the sentiments of Zach Weinberg. We just didn't know for sure. So why were liberal journalists focused on fear mongering by making misleading claims about a potential covid-19 treatment?

Remember CNN, NBC, and Bloomberg had all run stories with headlines attacking President Trump and his statements about hydroxychloroquine.

During this time, it wasn't just reporters and traditional news media outlets peddling fear and stamping out dissent. YouTube had also begun deplatforming videos related to covid-19 from several different channels. On May 18, 2020 UnHerd executive editor Freddie Sayers interviewed British physician Karol Sikora. Sikora had literally been a director with the WHO and Dean of Medicine at the University of Buckingham. During the 30-minute interview Sikora suggests that the virus is showing signs of slowing down because of social distancing, and more importantly herd immunity. Sikora also opined that fear of the virus is deadlier than the physical impact virus. These dissenting ideas didn't sit well with YouTube and the video featuring a literal medical doctor was banned. YouTube claimed the video was 'violating guidelines' as the reason for the removal. On May 21, 2020 after public backlash on Twitter, YouTube reinstated the video. Freddie Sayers had this to say:

> *"Ta da! @YouTube reinstates our*
> *@ProfKarolSikora interview - no doubt*
> *persuaded by the huge negative attention they*
> *were getting on here, so thanks Twitterers*
> *[peace symbol]*
>
> *For people without noisy friends, this kind of*
> *big tech censorship is the end of the road.*
> *Scary."* - @freddiesayers, May 21, 2020

Sayers is right, this type of censorship that silenced a medical doctor for giving their professional medical opinion is dangerous. But why would YouTube ban a video where a literal medical doctor, who had worked as a director for the World Health Organization who was giving his professional opinion? Curious.

UnHerd weren't the only ones whose content was being targeted for censorship. Full Measure News had their content removed from YouTube as well. A report by Sharyl Attkisson, host of the TV show, *Full Measure,* was removed by YouTube because they called it 'dangerous'. What was so dangerous? Attkinsson had interviewed Dr. William O'Neill who had this to say about the drug hydroxychloroquine:

> *"...President Trump touted it early, and so then the media set out to disprove and discredit it, without any regard for science. I think those of us that are actually involved in the scientific endeavor feel that there is some value to it, and it has to be tested."* - Dr. William O'Neill, May 17, 2020

Eventually YouTube reinstated the story claiming the removal was a mistake. Attkisson noted the video was only removed after complaints were lodged that it was putting people at risk. Who was complaining? A group called Media Matters. If the name sounds familiar, they're one of the organizations that is accused of paying people to harass the former reddit forum, r/the_donald. They are a self-described liberal organization and appear to be dedicated to pushing liberal media narratives. In that effort, Media Matters published an article on May 18, 2020 written by Bobby Lewis. In it Lewis claims that the Full Measure report, *"downplayed deaths among covid-19 patients who took hydroxychloroquine"*. Lewis closes his article accusing Full Measure of spreading misinformation when he states:

> *"(the) May 17 show wasn't the conservative broadcast company's first brush with coronavirus misinformation; [Attkisson's] Sinclair colleague Eric Bolling has spread conspiracy theories and right-wing talking points about the pandemic to viewers of his America This Week, while the network has also produced news segments leaving out warnings from experts and dishonestly defending Trump's boasts about his administration's response."*

It should be noted that Bobby Lewis holds a bachelor's degree in U.S. history from Ohio University, per the Media Matters website. Dr. O'Neill earned his medical degree in 1977 from Wayne State University, he is the Medical Director for the Center for Structural Heart Disease in Detroit, and is board certified by the American Board of Internal Medicine. One of these individuals is more qualified to provide comment about a public health crisis, during a public health crisis.

By May 20, 2020 YouTube relented and Atkisson tweeted that they had reinstated her report. In response to the removal Atkisson gave this statement to Sinclair Broadcast Group:

> *"...the incident highlights the increasingly narrowing of our information universe by self-appointed third parties who are often influenced or controlled by corporate and political interests that do not have the general public's best interests at heart. For example, Facebook has improperly flagged another Full Measure investigation as false when users have shared it, and many other internet users besides Full Measure have experienced their own brushes with censorship ... they often use their fake fact checks to hide accurate, factual information or viewpoints they do not wish the public to hear or consider."*

Atkisson also had this to say about the incident in a statement given to Daniel Payne at Just the News:

> *"It's very frightening because I feel like if something's not done, in five years, we're going to be telling our kids, 'There was once a time we could get any information we wanted on the internet.' That's changing. We can't anymore."*

Atkisson is exactly right in both of her statements. The fact that YouTube can silence dissenting viewpoints so easily should be frightening to everyone. Particularly if they're willing to silence medical experts who are commenting on a serious public health emergency. There are numerous more examples, but the most egregious censorship was being perpetrated against legitimate medical professionals. This included pulmonologist Roger Seheult. Dr. Seheult runs a YouTube channel called MedCram. He had been posting videos of covid-19 lectures since January 2020, and then abruptly on May 17, 2020 YouTube began removing some of his content. With no warning or explanation, five of his videos were deleted. Two of those deleted videos discussed hydroxychloroquine, and one discussed Remdesivir. The doctor appealed the decision and public outcry against the removal grew. Once again, YouTube relented. In a response given to Mark Bergen of Bloomberg news, YouTube stated:

> *"With the massive volume of videos on our site, sometimes we make the wrong call. When it's brought to our attention that a video has been removed mistakenly, we act quickly to reinstate it."*

When is censorship of medical professionals discussing legitimate medical issues the right call? YouTube's war on dissenting viewpoints has real world consequences, and likely won't improve. If YouTube is willing to silence the voices of medical professionals during a public health crisis, potentially jeopardizing lives, YouTube will certainly be willing to silence dissent to achieve their political goals.

Then on July 27, 2020 the country went haywire. A video was posted on YouTube by a group called, America's Frontline Doctors. In the video the group claims that hydroxychloroquine is an effective treatment for covid-19 symptoms as well as being an effective prophylaxis. Who were the people making these claims? Individuals with more education and training than a bachelor's degree in U.S. history might provide. The list included:

Dr. Simone Gold: emergency and general practice physician registered with the California Medical Board.

Dr. Joseph Ladapo: physician and clinical researcher at the University of California, Los Angeles.

Dr. Daniel Erickson: emergency medicine doctor who graduated from the Western University of Health Sciences.

Dr. Bob Hamilton: earned his bachelor's degree in biochemistry from UC Davis and attended UCLA for medical school and pediatric residency.

Dr. Stella Immanuel: graduated from the Nigerian medical school at the University of Calabar and completed a pediatric residency at the Bronx-Lebanon Hospital Center.

These are medical doctors, having earned all the rights, and privileges associated with the title. While their opinions may be unpopular or even incorrect, silencing a group of trained medical professionals is disturbing. But that's exactly what almost every media outlet did. After months of touting the line, "listen to the experts" it seemed the line had become "silence all dissent". The press conference video featuring AFD was immediately banned. President Trump retweeted a few versions of the video on his Twitter account before they were taken down. The corporate media machine began spinning the story that President Trump was undermining efforts to prevent the spread of covid-19. Don Jr. also tweeted the video and was immediately punished by Twitter. For the sin of sharing information provided by medical doctors, Donald Trump Jr. had his Twitter account suspended for 12 hours. Twitter gave the following statement as justification for the suspension:

> *"the removal of content that may pose a risk to people's health, including content that goes directly against guidance from authoritative sources of global and local public health information."*

Again, the AFD video featured numerous trained, medical professionals with decades of experience treating patients. Why are they not regarded as medical experts? Facebook, Twitter, Instagram, YouTube, they all banded together and colluded to keep a group of doctors from providing comments on their personal experience with treating covid-19. The hashtag #hydroxychloroquineworks became a top trending Twitter topic the following morning. Twitter launched their disinformation campaign by adding this statement under the topic:

> *"is not an effective treatment for covid-19, according to the FDA."*

The situation escalated when corporate media journalists began running hit pieces in an attempt at character assassination. Within 24 hours, every statement any of them had ever made was under scrutiny. The worst was how the liberal media treated Dr. Immanuel. While she has made some outrageous claims in the past, it doesn't discount her work with covid-19 patients. Yet, because of her more outlandish claims, the orange man bad gang made her the face of AFD. Journalists everywhere were intentionally ignoring the decades of experience represented by the contingent of doctors. The concern here is less about the position that any individual or group of doctors takes, but the approach taken by both digital tech companies, and traditional media outlets. It's concerning because there was a time when this same industry supported and profiteered off the narrative that medical doctors recommended and prescribed cigarettes. For nearly 20 years leading up to the 1950's everybody knew cigarettes were healthy. Afterall over

20,000 physicians recommended Lucky Strikes. Turns out inhaling smoke is terrible for the lungs.

The campaign of censorship and information control wasn't limited to just the treatment of covid-19, it also impacted the narrative on how covid-19 could spread. The draconian lockdowns implemented by many states were in full effect throughout the summer of 2020. At the same time several high-profile police shootings occurred that became flashpoints for civil unrest, looting, arson, and riots. Black Lives Matter and antifa lead the charge in their attempts to destabilize the country already experiencing a public health crisis.

While most of the country was on board with remain at home orders for a few weeks, when democratic governors made it clear they had no intentions of relinquishing the power they had seized people began pushing back. Around the middle of April 2020, lockdown protests had been organized in many U.S. states. These were peaceful protests, with no rioting, looting, or arson. The rallies and protests were collections of people exercising their first amendment right to peaceably assemble. The backlash from liberal media was immediate. Headlines began cropping up about conservative groups tied to President Trump were behind these movements. They were correct. An article was published by Reuters on April 21, 2020 titled, *How Trump allies have organized and promoted anti-lockdown protests.* In it the article even lambasts President Trump when they time the protest organizers to the White House:

> *"Republican politicians and individuals affiliated with President Donald Trump's re-election campaign are organizing or promoting anti-lockdown protests across key electoral battleground states, despite the White House's own cautious guidance on relaxing restrictions..."* - Michael Martina, Jarrett Renshaw, Tim Reid, April 21, 2020 via Reuters

There was an onslaught of condemnation by the orange man bad gang. An article published by PhillyMag is titled, *People Protesting Coronavirus Lockdown Orders Are Terrorists*. In it the writer, Ernest Owens states:

> *"Although there were no deaths at Monday's protest in Harrisburg, the protesters' spread of health misinformation (and, y'know, likely the virus), to say nothing of their demands to reopen the Commonwealth even as their neighbors continue to test positive and die, is endangering countless lives. Let's call it what it is: These lockdown protesters are acting as terrorists."* - Ernest Owens, April 21, 2020 via PhillyMag

Despite the poor grammar, their message is clear: protesting unconstitutional lockdowns is an act of terrorism. Owens wasn't the only one. Liberals across the board shared similar sentiments about the protestors:

> *"Meet COVIDIOTS-2, the second wave of stupidity amid the coronavirus crisis"* - Brian Niemietz, April 24, 2020 via New York Daily News

> *"These People Aren't Freedom Fighters They're Virus-Spreading Sociopaths"* - Elie Mystal, April 21, 2020 via The Nation

> *"I don't know any other way to characterize it, when we have an order from governors, both Republicans and Democrats, that basically are designed to protect people's health, literally their lives, to have a president of the United States basically encourage insubordination, to encourage illegal activity. These orders actually are the law of these states."* - Washington Democratic Governor Jay Inslee, April 19, 2020 via FoxNews

*"The whiteness of anti-lockdown protests: How
ignorance, privilege, and anti-black racism is
driving white protesters to risk their lives." -*
Maia Niguel Hoskin, APril 25, 2020 via Vox

*"These demonstrations reached an ugly peak
in Michigan last month though they may yet
worsen as the pandemic persists when armed
protesters rushed into the capitol building, and
put on a chilling display of fury and
intimidation. They claimed to be exercising their
democratic rights of free speech and gun
ownership. But there is something profoundly
undemocratic about this form of
demonstration." -* Firmin DeBrabander, May
13, 2020 via the Atlantic

*"These protests, they do undermine the effort,
and it's very clearly a political statement that is
playing out where people are coming together
from across the state, they are congregating,
they're not wearing masks, they are not
staying six feet apart, and then they go back
home into communities and the risk of
perpetuating the spread of covid-19 is real" -*
Democratic Governor of Michigan, Gretchen
Whitmer, May 13, 2020 via The View

These headlines and commentary were directed at people
who peacefully assembled. There was no looting. No stores
were burned to the ground. There was no vandalism. No
lives were lost. No assaults on the elderly. These were
peaceful protests. That didn't seem to matter. Even worse
there was state sanctioned religious persecution and
antisemitism when democratic New York City Mayor Bill de
Blasio sent out this series of tweets:

*"Something absolutely unacceptable happened
in Williamsburg tonite: a large funeral*

*gathering in the middle of this pandemic. When
I heard, I went there myself to ensure the
crowd was dispersed. And what I saw WILL
NOT be tolerated so long as we are fighting the
Coronavirus"* - @NYCMayor, April 28, 2020

*"My message to the Jewish community, and all
communities, is this simple: the time for
warnings has passed. I have instructed the
NYPD to proceed immediately to summons or
even arrest those who gather in large groups.
This is about stopping this disease and saving
lives. Period."* - @NYCMayor, April 28, 2020

Despite the right to peaceably assemble, to exercise
religious beliefs, to petition the government to redress
grievances all these people were willing to label protestors
as terrorists. Bill de Blasio was willing to threaten jail time
for those mourning the loss of a loved one. It was a
sickening display of governmental abuse of power and a
dark time for civil rights in the U.S.

Not wanting to miss out on the opportunity to silence
conservatives, Facebook stepped into the controversy. On
April 20, 2020 Facebook began removing protest events
organized on their platform. Protest events organized for
California, New Jersey, and Nebraska were all taken down.
Facebook issued a statement attempting to defend their
actions:

*"...events that defy government's guidance on
social distancing aren't allowed on Facebook"*

Facebook admits to working directly with government
officials to determine if a protest event should be removed.
Facebook released a statement saying that they were
consulting with lawmakers in New York, Ohio,
Pennsylvania, and Wisconsin to determine if lockdown
protests planned in those states should be removed. What a
time to be alive.

Cut to May 25, 2020. Career criminal George Floyd died while in police custody. While his death appears to have been completely unnecessary, he likely died of a combination of drug use noted by the toxicology report, poor health condition, and negligence by the arresting officers. In the numerous videos available, the arresting officers appear to have acted willfully negligent while detaining a suspect. There are two facts that drive my view of this terrible situation. The first being, George Floyd was a violent career criminal who previously robbed a woman at gunpoint. His life should not be celebrated. The second, and I'll say it louder for the people in the back, **police officers are not in place to act as judge, jury, and executioner.** When their duties require it, their responsibility to American citizens is to take people into custody using the least force possible. Sometimes it ends in tragedy when they are forced to take a life. However, kneeling on a man's neck for an extended amount of time is wildly unnecessary. I've trained Brazilian jiu jitsu for 4 years, and while I'm terrible at the sport, I know for fact it takes much less to effectively restrain a full-grown man. I know this because I'm usually the person being restrained, and usually by someone much smaller, and not nearly as strong as me.

But people were out of work, schools were shut down, everyone's future was uncertain, and every news media outlet was inciting a culture of fear and panic in their audience. George Floyd's death was the spark that lit the tinderbox. People were right to be angry. They were right to protest. They were right to demand police reforms. They were not right to loot stores, burn down buildings, viciously attack people, shoot law enforcement officers, or riot for the next 3 months. But that's just the background for what came next. In a report published by The Hastings Center, the author's pose their question in the title, *Are Physicians Hypocrites for Supporting Black Lives Matter Protests and Opposing Anti-Lockdown Protests?* That headline really says it all. The authors go on to say:

> *"...there are legitimate reasons for viewing the anti-lockdown and Black Lives Matter protests differently both from a medical and a societal perspective. The most straightforward argument is that the purpose of the anti-lockdown protests is diametrically opposite to medical recommendations while the Black Lives Matter demands are consistent with public health imperatives."* - Bjorg Thorsteinsdottir, P. Preston Reynolds, Lisa Rucker, Elizabeth Dzeng & Randy Goldberg, August 27, 2020

Gaslighting at its finest, and it wasn't just liberal activists and journalists engaging in this type of divisive behaviour. Remember democratic governor Gretchen Whitmer? On June 4, 2020, just three weeks after condemning lockdown protests, she was photographed kneeling at a black lives matter protest, in a mass of people, none of them socially distanced, and many not wearing masks. Similar photo opportunities were shared by Bill DeBlasio, Tom Wolf, Phil Murphy, and many other democratic politicians. All of them taking the time to join BLM marches across the country having spent the previous months condemning lockdown protests on the grounds they were spreading covid-19. It was peak hypocrisy and typified politics in 2020.

In addition to terrible leadership displayed by democratic politicians, Facebook piled on. Just weeks earlier the very same company that was deleting organized efforts to protest the lockdown, began openly promoting BLM and their protests. Black Lives Matter Philly was allowed to organize the following in person events on Facebook:

> *June 26*
> *We Want Freedom For Black Philly Press Conference*
> *Fri 11 AM · 1,064 guests*
> *600 Market St, Philadelphia, PA 19106-2310, United States*

June 20
SayHERName March for Justice
Sat 1 PM · 1,530 guests
56th & Chestnut Street

June 19
Jawnteenth
Fri 4 PM · 4,084 guests
Malcolm X Park
Philadelphia

June 13
Protest Philadelphia Police Terrorism
Sat 12 PM · 3,180 guests
6221 Osage Avenue
Philadelphia

June 7
Free People Now!
Sun 1 PM · 2,382 guests
Eastern State Penitentiary
Philadelphia

May 30
Solidarity Against Police Terrorism
Sat 2 PM · 6,166 guests
Philadelphia Museum of Art
Philadelphia

Doing so in defiance of state orders they had previously cited for the removing lockdown protest events. New York, Pennsylvania, California, and New Jersey all had numerous BLM protest events organized during the months of unrest. These were all states that Facebook had worked with to remove lockdown protest events.

This isn't a game of some protests are valid, and some are not, the first amendment was quoted towards the beginning of this chapter for a reason. Both lockdown protests and BLM protests should have been treated with respect. American citizens enjoy the rights enshrined by the bill of rights. Arguing against either the BLM protests or the lockdown protests is pure tribalism. When journalists compile lists of people practicing their religion, referring to religious leaders as COVIDIOTS in one breath, and hailing BLM protestors in the next it is troubling. When news media outlets, journalists, and digital technology platforms selectively censor which voices are allowed to speak, they contribute to the loss of America's most deeply held values. Moreover, they shift from being reliable sources of information to simply being disinformants.

chapter 10: internet killed all the other stars

Video may have killed the radio star, but the internet killed all the rest. There's no denying the fact that the rise of the internet has had a massive impact on the way humanity accesses information. The first wave to fall victim were the things most vulnerable to the rise of digital technology including books, magazines, newspapers, and mail. Email slowly began to supplant first class, or letter mail. In 2000 first class mail delivery volume peaked at over 103 billion parcels. In 2019 that number had shrunk to just under 55 billion, the lowest number since 1977. Printed and hardbound encyclopedias had been slowly supplanted by digital versions in the early 1990s, online encyclopedias became popularized by Wikipedia when it launched in 2001. By 2016 it was estimated that Wikipedia had more than 18 billion views per month in traffic. As information became more widely available online, people spent less and less time in libraries. Google Books library project launched in 2004 hastening their fall. The University of Toronto estimates from 2000 through 2015 annual visitors to their library dropped from around 4.5 million per year to less than 2 million per year. Amazon launched the Kindle and The Kindle Store in 2007 bringing portable ebooks available away from desktop computers. They were sold out in less than 6 hours. File sharing popularized by Napster launched an entire wave of innovation in the music industry, reshaping music sales from record stores to digital downloads, to streaming services. Just as tapes replaced records, and CDs replaced tapes, the iPod replaced cd players which in turn were replaced by the iPhone. Streaming services like Pandora and Spotify are replacing music radio services, and podcasts are replacing radio shows.

Website news resources contributed to the decline of printed media, more easily delivered via the internet. Newspaper advertising revenue has dropped from an estimated revenue peak in 2000 of over $60 billion dollars, to less than $15 billion by 2017. In 2008 newspapers employed over 70 thousand people with over 55 million daily newspapers circulated. By 2018 those numbers had dropped to around 34 thousand employees and 28 million daily newspapers. In March 2020, Playboy announced they would no longer be issuing their monthly magazine in print form, after 66 years. Border's bookstore once boasted over 30,000 employees and over $2 billion USD in revenue in 1996, filed for bankruptcy in 2011. Craigslist, ebay, Indeed, and LinkedIn all replaced the classified, want ads, and job listings formerly printed in newspapers. While not dead, almost every company in the print media industry has seen reductions in revenue and depth.

The internet came for movie rentals with the rise of Netflix. They killed Blockbuster, a company they had tried to partner with in 2000 for $50 million USD. That year Blockbuster's revenue topped $4.9 billion. For a little more than 1% of their total revenue that year, society could have had blockbuster and bang. Netflix is now valued at around $190 billion dollars. Similarly, videotapes were supplanted by DVD and then Blu-ray, only to be replaced by streaming and digital download options from cable companies, Amazon, Netflix, Hulu, Disney+, and AppleTV.

Brick and mortar retail declines started next with the rise of Amazon. Amazon, which started as an online book retailer is credited for ending Borders mentioned earlier. Amazon is also credited for killing Toys "R" Us, Sears, and countless others. In reality it's probably just a shift away from super specialty stores selling one category of items, into super, super stores, that sell everything. This is evidenced by the rise of super Walmarts, super Targets, and Amazon's own push into brick and mortar spaces with their acquisition of Whole Foods. Coupled with the great recession in 2008, and shifting demographics showing a migration back into urban cities, the large megamalls that had dominated the suburban landscape were being supplanted by online shopping, and Walmart super centers. Without the foot traffic in malls, boutique brand specific shops struggled, and when covid-19 lockdowns rolled out across the country in spring of 2020 companies like J.

Crew, JCPenney, Neiman Marcus, Sur La Table, Lord & Taylor, and GNC all filed for bankruptcy.

The third wave coincided with the delivery of smartphones, and the rise of subscription based digital fee structures. Spotify launched their app in 2008 and opened paid subscription to everyone. Sony PlayStation Plus launched in 2010. But it wasn't until the rise of the smartphone that internet access became the dominant technology to deliver information. GameStop has been in steady decline since 2013. Their revenue losses are stacking up due in part to digital downloads for video games through services like PlayStation Plus, and with covid-19 lockdowns still in place, their future is uncertain. Uber and Lyft have mortally wounded taxis. Remember the taxi protests around the world as Uber expanded their operating markets? At their peak in 2013 a taxicab medallion in New York City was valued at over $1 million USD. Six years later a public auction sold just 3 out of 16 medallions for an average of $137 thousand USD. All these industries have been reshaped by the internet, sometimes from the foundation up. As traditional businesses play catch up with the changes technology has brought, these impacts will become less frequent and present a less disruptive threat, until the next wave of radical new technology. Journalism, as an industry, is no different.

Far more agile than most industries journalism has been able to adapt fairly well to the new digital world. Currently they are experiencing a glut of journalists all writing for various online versions of their former print media companies. But the power of journalism in society is alive and well. People clamor for the latest news, gossip, rumors, tech updates, secrets, and scandals. Technology only diffuses that power enabling daily commuters to become front-line journalists at a moment's notice. The rise of the video camera smartphone allows almost everyone to be their own self-contained reporter and camera crew news team. Crowd sourced videos have been a part of many major news stories carried by corporate media outlets, and it only seems to be increasing. This downward pressure on the journalism industry mentioned earlier is likely having a short term, direct, and negative impact on the quality and ethical standards within the industry. However, I believe it will ultimately result in a healthier, and more responsible ecosystem of journalism and reporting. Take for example the story of the New York Times reporter pushing salacious rumors about First Lady Melania Trump. Emily Ratajkowski sent out two tweets on February 13, 2017 that called out the New York Times. In 45 words and less than a minute she was able to break a story that forced the New York Times to issue an apology. That would never have happened, and the world wouldn't have known about it without the power of Twitter. This type of responsive and public fact checking, and correction will force the industry to adapt, if it's not stamped out by digital tech companies seeking to expand their role as thought police, exercising unbounded and biased censorship.

The same power of the internet that forced the New York Times to hold their journalists accountable is what led to the eventual downfall of Bill Cosby for his vicious history of rape and sexual abuse. Nobody in traditional journalism was willing to run the story of Cosby's proclivity for raping young women. Even though early allegations of Cosby's predatory behaviour were being shared as far back as the 1980s they went largely ignored. Joan Tarshis claims she told her story to a journalist in 1980 who refused to publish it. In a taped interview in 1996, a woman named Victoria Valentino made allegations that Cosby had drugged and raped her. In 2000, Lachele Covington claimed she was sexually assaulted by Cosby and reported it to the NYPD with no charges filed. In 2002 Janice Dickinson wrote about being raped by Cosby in her autobiography but her publisher wouldn't publish the allegations over legal concerns. In 2005 Therese Serignese accused Cosby of rape and Cosby was forced to admit under oath that he did in fact give her Quaaludes. Cosby wasn't charged. Also, in 2005 Andrea Constand was sexually assaulted, and again Cosby was forced to admit under oath the incident occured but claimed it was consensual. Again, Cosby was not charged. The list goes on but for more than 25 years these allegations were ignored by traditional media outlets.

It took until 2014 when comedian Hannibal Buress was performing in Philadelphia for traditional media outlets to take notice. During part of his set Buress was addressing Cosby's admonitions to the black community about sagging pants and having children out of wedlock. During this segment, Buress criticized the actor as a hypocrite and stated:

"Yeah, but you raped women, Bill Cosby, so that kind of brings you down a couple notches."

Sensing the audience was stunned, Buress encouraged everyone to search 'Bill Cosby rape' on Google. Even though Buress had been talking about Cosby raping women for more than six months, it wasn't until it was posted in an article on Philadelphia magazine's website that the story grew legs. This was thanks in large part to people using Google to search up relevant news stories, and the website article. People began to take notice.

On November 10, 2014 Bill Cosby's Twitter account posted a photo inviting the internet to meme him. It was a massive backfire as the internet rose up and used it to highlight sexual assault allegations made against him. Then on November 30, 2014 Salon was courageous enough to publish an article that discussed the allegations of sexual assault involving Bill Cosby. The next month Vanity Fair published an article featuring Beverly Johnson who alleged Cosby had drugged her during an audition in the 1980s. By July 2015 more than 30 women had come forward making accusations against Cosby. That month New York magazine featured a cover with 35 women sitting and willing to tell their story of being assaulted by Bill Cosby. But why did it take until 2015 for this story to break? Corporate media was forced to break the wall of silence they had created by a young comedian, the rising power and influence of Twitter, and the internet.

The ever-increasing role of the internet, and social media in breaking stories makes sense. With the ease of uploading videos of tornadoes, hurricanes, and other emergencies, every citizen with a smartphone can be a front-line reporter, getting news out to the world at a moment's notice. In 2011, more than 40 thousand tweets were sent out in the first minute of an earthquake that shook the D.C. area. This was 30 minutes before anyone in mainstream corporate media knew what was happening. In 2009 photos of a plane crashing into the Hudson River were captured by a twitter user.

> *"There's a plane in the Hudson. I'm on the ferry going to pick up the people. Crazy."* - @jkrums, January 15, 2009

That crash later became known as the *Hudson River Miracle*, with pilots Chesley Sullenberger and Jeffrey Skiles, and their brave crew being credited for saving the lives of all passengers that day. In an industry measured by how fast you can report a breaking story, it's tough to compete with a world filled with pocket sized camera crews and the ability to upload real time videos.

Nowhere is this more evident than in Hong Kong where millions of citizens marched for freedom against a tyrannical communist regime. In 2019, leaders in Hong Kong proposed an amendment bill called the Fugitive Offenders amendment bill. Under the guise of closing legal loopholes, the Hong Kong government was proposing changes that would allow extradition to jurisdictions such as mainland China and the ruling Chinese Communist Party. This is a worry because the Chinese Communist Party regularly disappears, imprisons, and murders political dissidents, Christians, Muslims, and anyone that challenges the Communist Party. It was a direct attack on the citizens of Hong Kong and a direct threat to their civil liberties. Fearing that Hong Kong residents, and visitors would be subject to the capricious legal system of mainland China and communist tyranny, Hong Kong citizens began to protest. These political protests began on March 15, 2019 when a sit-in at the government headquarters was staged. On June 9, 2019, an estimated million people marched in protest. In an effort to stall the bill in Hong Kong's legislative procedure protestors gathered outside the

Legislative Council Complex on June 12, 2019. This protest escalated into violence initiated by foot soldiers of the oppressive communist regime.

Consistent throughout the protests was the use of cell phone video footage both live streamed, and uploads. These images and videos were put on display for the world to see, and free people around the globe showed their support for the people of Hong Kong. While many local affiliates of international news outlets did provide some coverage, one thing was clear, traditional news corporations couldn't compete with crowdsourced journalism. As we see the rise of divisive and misleading journalism, the more important question might be, are they even willing to?

The NBA banned fans and signs showing support for the Hong Kong protestors. In October 2019, Houston Rockets' general manager Daryl Morey was criticized for supporting Hong Kong protesters. Both the Chinese Communist Party and basketball fans wanted him fired. The league pressured a feckless Morey into an apology. Yet just a few months later political messaging in the form of BLM was not only allowed but featured on the court. It's a glaring display of hypocrisy. But the NBA is big business, and with the league in bed with the Chinese Communist Party it made sense to let marxists pull their strings.

CNN, MSNBC, FoxNews are also big businesses with investors and advertisers they answer too. But as news media companies they also are inexorably tied to and viewed as sources of journalism. Where do these companies draw the line between revenue and ethics? Like most businesses it's likely only when they are forced to. Sensationalism sells and pushing the orange man bad narrative is easy money in a world filled with corporations cowed by the woke mob. What about when their allies are venomous predators? Recent stories show television personalities and the orange man bad crew were complicit in covering up for criminals like Harvey Weinstein, Bill Cosby, and other monsters who towed the party line.

In February 2020, Hillary Clinton was attending the Berlin International Film Festival. At one-point Clinton was asked about Weinstein contributing to her 2016 presidential campaign. Hillary's response:

> *"He contributed to every Democrat's campaign."*

Shockingly, she wasn't lying this time. According to the Center for Responsive Politics, Harvey Weinstein and his family donated more than $1.4 million USD to political campaigns dating back to 1992. Virtually all the money went towards funding the Democratic Party. It took until October 2017 for two reporters, Jodi Kantor and Megan Twohey, for any major news outlet to report that dozens of women over a 30-year period had accused Harvey Weinstein of rape, sexual assault and sexual abuse. Surely that means Harvey Weinsten was a criminal mastermind who was able to keep his wrongdoings a well-kept secret. Quite the opposite.

Rumors of Weinstein's sexual abuses had circulated in Hollywood for decades. During a 1998 appearance on the Late Show with David Letterman, actress Gwyneth Paltrow told Lettermen that Weinsten:

> *"...will coerce you to do a thing or two."*

Gwyneth wasn't the only one. In 2005 Courtney Love issued this dire warning:

> *"If Harvey Weinstein invites you to a private party in the Four Seasons, don't go."*

In 2010 Courtney Enlow wrote an article for Pajiba titled, *Harvey's Girls*. In it she states:

> *"Rumors of Harvey's casting couch ways are legendary."*

Also, in 2010 Ivana Lowell wrote a book titled, *Why Not Say What Happened?* In it she wrote about Weinsten's inappropriate behaviour. In 2012, 30 Rock turned Weinstein's crimes into a joke when the following line was given to the character Jenna Maroney:

"I'm not afraid of anyone in show business, I turned down intercourse with Harvey Weinstein on no less than three occasions, out of five."

In 2013 during an award show Seth MacFarlane made a joke saying:

"Congratulations, you five ladies no longer have to pretend to be attracted to Harvey Weinstein."

It was openly talked about, and even more sickening, it was joked about by people for decades. For a movie mogul as big as Weinstein, why did nobody write about it? Why were there no journalists or publishers with the moral courage to write about the story? After the story broke the New York Times wrote:

"If Mr. Weinstein built his wall of invulnerability from many varied bricks, it was covered with a sheen of celebrity. He created stars through his movies, but he also acquired famous friends through his other activities, including in the Democratic politics that dominate Hollywood.

Chief among them were Bill and Hillary Clinton. Over the years, Mr. Weinstein provided them with campaign cash and Hollywood star power, inviting Mrs. Clinton to glittery premieres and offering to send her films. After Mr. Clinton faced impeachment in the Monica Lewinsky scandal, he donated $10,000 to Mr. Clinton's legal defense fund. Mr. Weinstein was a fund-raiser and informal adviser during Mrs.

> *Clinton's 2000 Senate campaign, a guest in her hotel suite when she won and a host of an A-list victory party. He was an early backer of both her presidential bids."*

Apparently, Clinton's loss in 2016 was enough to shake loose the story and Jodi Kantor and Megan Twohey were able to publish their story.

How do we know the media machine was complicit in covering up for such a prolific democratic political donor? Because in 2015 The New York Times published an article that reported Weinstein had been questioned by police about a sexual assault. Why didn't it go anywhere? Weinstein had been accused by Ambra Gutierrez of inappropriately touching her. She cooperated with the New York City Police Department throughout the investigation and was able to obtain audio recorded evidence of Weinstein admitting to the assault. The media machine went into action. Publishers ran negative stories about Gutierrez in an attempt to assassinate her character. It was perpetrated by the same people who had suppressed Rose McGowan's allegations. Even more disappointing was the lack of law enforcement action. Then Manhattan District Attorney Cyrus Vance Jr. declined to file charges against Weinstein, citing insufficient evidence of criminal intent. To quote Jill Stein, *"the fix was in."*

Society has Jodi Kantor and Megan Twohey, and the victims willing to speak up, to thank for a prolific sexual predator being brought to justice. Their tenacity inspired millions of other people to come forward when the #metoo movement was born. On October 15, 2017 Alyssa Milano tweeted out:

> *"If you've been sexually harassed or assaulted write 'me too' as a reply to this tweet."* - @Alyssa_Milano, October 15, 2017

There was an accompanying photo with the words:

> *Me too.*

Suggested by a friend: "If all the women who have been sexually harassed or assaulted wrote 'Me too.' as a status we might give people a sense of the magnitude of the problem"

By noon the next day, #metoo had been tweeted or retweeted more than 500 thousand times. On Facebook #metoo was used by 4.7 million people in just 24 hours. But this movement to help millions of women wasn't born out of responsible corporate news media coverage of Harvey Weinstein. They had decades to act and yet they stood by silently. Nor was it the Hollywood machine, who's very stars joked openly about Weinstein's proclivities. No, the #metoo movement was born on Twitter, and Facebook. The will of the people was what made it newsworthy. The millions of people who tweeted, and retweeted it, liked, and shared it broke this story. While the movement has had its share of baseless witch hunts, it is tough to deny the positive impact it has had in forcing traditional news media outlets to finally start reporting on the monsters in power who were previously being shielded from scrutiny by corporate media journalists.

Why do I say this? Because the phrase "me too" started on Myspace in 2006. A community organizer named Tarana Burke began using the phrase "me too" as a way to promote "empowerment through empathy" for women of color who have been sexually assaulted. Burke said "me too" was inspired by a conversation with a 13-year-old girl who confided to her that she had been sexually abused. Why wasn't it newsworthy in 2006 when Tarana Burke shared her story? Where was CNN, Slate, Vox, or FoxNews when Gwenyth Paltrow, or Courtney Love, or Seth MacFarlane talked about it? Why didn't MSNBC, the Atlantic, or the Huffington Post report on Weinstein when Ambra Gutierrez had evidence and a taped confession she was assaulted? Because corporate news media had made a choice that their ethical responsibility as journalists and publishers to report the news was subordinate to being a business first. I hold no sympathy for corporate journalism as the internet slowly supplants them with the rise of crowdsourced journalism. Like a forest fire cleaning out the deadwood, my hope is that technology will allow for a renaissance of ethical reporting. My only fear is that companies like Twitter, Facebook, reddit, and Google will rise in their place as information gatekeepers to keep the disinformation machine alive.

chapter 11: fake news

Fake news is not always politically motivated, for some it's big business. Stories of teenagers in the Balkans using clickbait to make upwards of $10,000 USD in a single day during election season filled the pages of Buzzfeed. I guess they hate the competition. But there is admittedly many fake news sites on the internet designed solely for making money. It turns out the best way to fish with clickbait is politics, American politics. Facebook admits a click from a Facebook user from America is worth more per click than one from any other country. Facebook has also acknowledged that people are more likely to interact with posts that evoke a negative emotional response. Combine all these with a politically divided nation, add some spicy headlines, and voilà, ad revenue. Since the 2016 election Facebook has worked towards eliminating this type of content. One of the ways it has done this is their fact checking initiative mentioned in chapter 6. But as with all bureaucracies, mission creep pushed the boundaries for the Ministry of Facts and their efforts expanded from removing stories linking Hillary Clinton with zombie cults, to editorializing, and in some egregious cases, outright lying.

Fact checkers do perform actual fact checks without bias on occasion. The researchers going to great length to calibrate their analysis of facts to mitigate any personal beliefs and present a whole view of the topic. But more often fact checking is skewed towards one world view or another. This bias generally stems from the author's own internal bias, or the cultural bias within the company performing the fact check. The current trend in bias veers heavily left. What does this look like to an objective reader? One example is Joe Biden. His self-avowed gaffe machine never seems to sleep, and so he often makes incorrect, and inappropriate statements. Those statements are sometimes identified as false by PolitiFact, Snopes, or FactCheck.org. However, when a conservative makes a gaffe it is always identified, in great detail, with supporting material. After all it's easy for a person to drag their feet on work they don't want to do and not fact checking the blue team is easily accomplished. But the bias is often more insidious than that. In at least one case dating back to 2012 it was crystal clear. In August of 2012 Ron Paul, a former U.S. Congressman, and conservative leaning Libertarian stated that the federal tax rate was 0% up until 1913. PolitiFact jumped on the story and rated it half true. Only three short years later, the former U.S. Senator, and registered democrat Jim Webb made the same claim on his campaign website stating, *"we did not even have a federal income tax in this country until 1913."* The PolitiFact ruling: mostly true. The hypocrisy is galling. It took until December 2016 for PolitiFact to issue this correction:

> *"Correction (Dec. 20, 2016): This fact-check initially published on Aug. 24, 2015 and was rated Mostly True. Upon reconsideration, we are changing our ruling to Half True. The text of the fact-check is unchanged."*

Chapter 6 discusses Facebook and their fact check crusade. It showed how a PolitiFact 'fact check' asserted President Trump had made a false statement, and I provided a counter argument that he clearly made a true statement. In this chapter I'm just going to give more examples of biased fact checking and fake news narratives pushed by their respective owners. There will be more detail and some analysis regarding fact checks that are clearly written with misleading headlines, and commentary on clearly biased journalism. Ultimately the journalists writing these fact checks and reporting on news will be representing their own level of professionalism, and it will be up to each person if they feel the fact check articles here are the real fake news.

Date: June 30, 2020
Publisher: USA Today
Writer: Devon Link
Headline: *Fact check: Democratic Party did not found the KKK, did not start the Civil War.*

In the article the author then posted a quote from an Instagram post, and goes on to mention the ensuing discussion surrounding the quote. It's not included here but the broad point was that democrats founded the KKK. Clearly the author disagrees on this point. However, later in the article Devon claims:

> *"Historians agree that although factions of the Democratic Party did **majorly** contribute to the Civil War's start and the KKK's founding, it is inaccurate to say the party is responsible for either."*

Author's note: **majorly** *- primarily, extremely.*
Additional note: I added the bold emphasis on majorly from the original quote.

Sure. Okay. If someone wants to thread that needle down the road of "well technically…". They would be right. Every democrat didn't join the klan. There were a few democrats who were outspoken abolitionists, but democrats in every other way. However, all the founding klansmen were democrats. Which says something. I'll leave it to the reader to decide exactly what that information says about the Democratic Party. As I mentioned before, it is not my role, nor the role of any company to decide how each person interprets information or if they shout it to the world. However, I'm sure in some way, the information here will shape a person's opinion, just like religious beliefs, our peers, our families, and our mentors all influence how we see the world.

Date: June 29, 2020
Publisher: USA Today
Writer: Sarah Lynch
Headline: *Fact check: Congress did not designate Confederate veterans as U.S. veterans.*

In this article the author posts a quote from a Facebook post, and the ensuing discussion surrounding the quote. Here the author cites the federal code, provides part of what the federal code states, and continues their diatribe. Again, here the author disagrees with the primary claim of the Facebook posting. Once again, later in the article the writer claims:

> *"This amendment to the Veterans' Benefit Act does indeed expand the definition of "veteran" to include "a person who served in the military or naval forces of the Confederate States of America during the Civil War." However, the act also clearly specifies that this inclusion applies "for the purpose of this section, and section 433," which Jessica Owley, professor of law at the University of Miami, interpreted as a limited extension."*

Maybe I'm confused. The title of the article was quite clear in the assertion that Congress, the legislative branch of the U.S. government, wholly responsible, with an oath bound duty, to write the laws governing our country, did NOT make Confederate soldiers veterans. Yet halfway through the article, the author also clearly states that yes, this amendment to the Veterans' Benefit Act does indeed expand the definition of a veteran to include Confederate soldiers.

Date: June 29, 2020
Publisher: Snopes
Writer: Nur Ibrahim
Headline: *Did Biden Say 120 Million People Had Died from covid-19?*

As the title implies, this article evaluates if democratic presidential nominee Joe Biden said 120 million people had died from covid-19 and rates it mostly false. The only trouble is, the author immediately goes on to state that Joe Biden said, *"Now we have over 120 million dead from covid,"* at a campaign event in Pennsylvania. To be fair Joe Biden does correct himself and continues by stating:

> *"I mean, 120 thousand dead from covid. And you have so many, now we're past 2 million. I mean, and we're talking about it like it's over. I mean, it's over. My god."*

Allegedly. The second quote is from audio released by the campaign as the video cuts out just after Biden's original statement. There's no way to tell if that audio is from the original campaign event or not.

Even PolitiFact has rated this story true. In their fact check article, the author confirms that Joe Biden had not only stated that 120 million people died of covid-19, but another 150 million died from gun violence. PolitiFact also points out Biden's correction of covid-19 deaths to the more accurate 120 thousand, but also fails to mention that he stumbles again, and says there's over 2 million.

So, did he mean 120 thousand, or 2 million? The follow up audio clip still leaves unanswered questions. Regardless, the original question stands. Joe Biden, for fact, on camera, with audio, stated that 120 million people had died from covid-19. At the very least this is a half true assertion. To rate it completely false, is completely false.

Date: September 15, 2020
Publisher: PolitiFact
Writer: Daniel Funke
Headline: *Tucker Carlson guest airs debunked conspiracy theory that COVID-19 was created in a lab*

Virologist Li-meng Yan gave an interview to Tucker Carlson on September 15, 2020. During her interview Dr. Yan claims covid-19 was genetically engineered by Chinese scientists on behalf of the Chinese Communist Party in a lab in Wuhan. Dr. Yan told Carlson:

> *"I can present solid scientific evidence to our audience that this virus, covid-19 SARS-CoV-2 virus, actually is not from nature. It is a man-made virus created in the lab."*

This theory is currently disputed by many doctors and scientists from around the globe. I lack the intelligence and general knowledge of virology to dispute any of their claims, including Dr. Yan. I'm reminded of Louis Pasteur, Georg Ohm, and John Yudkin. All discredited. All ultimately vindicated. That may or may not be the case here, but if she has evidence, it should be presented and examined. Time will tell if she is correct. It may very well be that she is incorrect, but she is a doctor, moreover she's a virologist with firsthand knowledge of covid-19. What is known is that she has co-authored two papers, one titled, *Viral dynamics in mild and severe cases of covid-19,* published March 19, 2020. A second paper titled, *Pathogenesis and transmission of SARS-CoV-2 in golden hamsters*, published May 14, 2020. Both papers were co-authored with fellow researchers at Hong Kong University where she worked as a virologist.

Humanity strays into dangerous territory when it silences all dissent, and once again that's what PolitiFact is attempting to do. It's not just PolitiFact, Facebook and Twitter have also taken measures to silence Dr. Yan. Twitter suspended Dr. Yan's account after her appearance on Tucker Carlson. Facebook and Instagram didn't take such drastic measures, they simply flagged the interview as false information. Quite frankly as of this writing the world doesn't know if Dr. Yan is correct, and if people aren't allowed to demand her findings be published and evaluated, we never will.

Date: August 20, 2020
Publisher: PolitiFact
Writer: Jill Terreri Ramos
Headline: *Cuomo ended cash bail … and now the crime rate has gone through the roof*

This writer gave President Trump a false rating for his statements regarding cash bail and crime rates in New York. President Trump claims Cuomo ended cash bail, and states in rebuttal:

> *"Statutory changes over how and when New York judges can impose cash bail took effect in January, with the intent of keeping people accused of certain crimes out of jail while they await trial, regardless of their ability to afford bail."*

Word salad, as later in their article the author writes:

> *"Cuomo signed changes to cash bail into law, but many violent felonies and other crimes, such as sex offenses, are still eligible for bail."*

So, Cuomo did effectively end cash bail for some crimes. He signed this legislation in 2019, and it became effective January 1, 2020. So, President Trump's statements are half true here. Or at least partially true. The second part of President Trump's statement regarding crime going through the roof can be easily shown. Crime statistics are published, and public knowledge. Statistics published by the New York Police Department on September 2, 2020 show that:

> *Murder is up +34% (291 v. 217) for the first eight months of 2020 when compared to the first eight months of 2019.*

*There were 242 citywide shooting incidents in
August 2020, compared to 91 shooting
incidents in August 2019, a +166% increase.*

*Year-to-date, through August 31, there is a
+87% spike in citywide shooting incidents
(1,014 v. 541).*

*Burglary increased +22% (1,310 v. 1,076) in
August and is up +42% (9,942 v. 7,008) year-
to-date through August 31.*

Those aren't all the crime categories listed, and some
categories of violent crime are down, including rape. But it's
tough to argue that New York hasn't seen a dramatic
increase in violent crime. Even the Wall Street Journal
agrees with President Trump. Writer Ben Chapman asks,
What's Fueling New York City's Rise in Violent Crime? The
article published on August 10, 2020 is where he states:

*"New York City has seen a surge in shootings
and other violent crime amid the new
coronavirus pandemic, but the factors driving
the trend are up for debate."*

Based on the crime stats, and other outside observers also
noticing the dramatic uptick in violent crime, this part of
President Trump's statement is also true, or mostly true.

PolitiFact correctly points out that New York
democratic leaders did fight to release many prisoners
under the guise of covid-19 safety measures, which also
could have also contributed to the increase in crime rates.
But even considering there's likely no objective way to
establish a cause and effect relationship for the changes to
bail in New York and the rise in crime, there's also no way
to prove the bail changes didn't have a direct impact on the
rise in crime. It would not be unfair to say President
Trump's statement here is half true. Cuomo did end cash
bail, and crime rates have increased dramatically
afterwards. Objectively this is not a false statement.

Date: August 25, 2020
Publisher: CNN
Writer: unknown
Headline: *Fiery But Mostly Peaceful Protests After Police Shooting*

2020 was a tumultuous year and the protests that occurred over the summer were a large part of that chaos. Earlier chapters have discussed the protests and riots in various democrat run cities. There were calls to defund the police led by democrat politicians, and the only voice of reason seemed to be conservative minded politicians. On the morning of August 25, 2020 CNN aired a clip featuring Omar Jimenez who was on the ground reporting from Kenosha, Wisconsin. The riots this time were in response to the shooting of career criminal Jacob Blake. While this shooting may or may not be justified, people in Kenosha were angry, bored, and ready to loot and burn down some neighborhoods. Omar Jimenez was there to report on the activities of the peaceful protestors. There were two interesting things viewers pointed out. The first was the fact that Omar was pontificating on how peaceful the protests were, while standing in front of the burning rubble of a store that had been destroyed by arsonists. The second interesting thing was the banner across the bottom of the screen that read, *"Fiery But Mostly Peaceful Protests After Police Shooting"*.

The clip went viral and was regarded as some of the most dishonest reporting about the civil unrest and rioting over the summer of 2020. The sad part is CNN wasn't the only news channel pushing this sad narrative. MSNBC was caught performing the same doublespeak. On May 29, 2020 when journalist Ali Velshi provided this commentary to Brian Williams on the riots in Minneapolis:

"I want to be clear on how I characterize this. This is mostly a protest. It is not, generally speaking, unruly but fires have been started and this crowd is relishing that."

He said this while on camera, standing in front of a building that had been set on fire by arsonists. How many fires had been started? He later admitted that he could see at least four different fires, including the 3rd precinct police department. For the record, arson is defined as:

"a crime of willfully and maliciously setting fire to or charring property. Though the act typically involves buildings, the term arson can also refer to the intentional burning of other things, such as motor vehicles, watercraft, or forests. The crime is typically classified as a felony, with instances involving a greater degree of risk to human life or property carrying a stricter penalty." - Wikipedia, September 2020

Arson is not a peaceful way to protest. It is not a peaceable way to assemble, and it is not a peaceable way to petition your government and redress grievances. It is a crime, that sometimes has deadly results. On July 21, 2020, a body was found in the burned down rubble of a pawn shop. Using video evidence, police arrested and charged a man named Montez Terriel Lee on June 11, 2020 for allegedly setting fire to the pawn shop on May 28. Minneapolis Police Department spokesman John Elder gave this statement to the Star Tribune:

"The body appears to have suffered thermal injury, and we do have somebody charged with setting fire to that place." - John Elder, July 21, 2020 via the Star Tribune

Even if some democrats want to make the case that arson is a form of peaceful protest, murder is not. If the autopsy shows the victim died as a result of the fire, that's exactly what it will be.

Date: September 17, 2020
Publisher: Poynter
Writer: Alex Mahadevan
Headline: *Here's how the Sturgis Motorcycle Rally's may have spread the coronavirus*

Remember the Poytner Institute mentioned in Chapter 6? They founded PolitiFact. On September 21, 2020 Poytner published an article by Alex Mahadevan that states that:

> *"A team of four researchers said the rally could be responsible for as many as 266,796 coronavirus cases in the U.S. over a month's time. About 19% of the cases reported between Aug. 2 and Sept. 2.*
>
> *The rally was a "superspreading event" with a hefty price tag because it combined many "worst case scenarios" for coronavirus spread, the researchers wrote.*
>
> *The preliminary report from San Diego State University's Center for Health Economics & Policy Studies estimated that the Sturgis-linked infections could have generated over $12 billion in health care costs."*

So far Poytner is spreading news from a report that claims the popular Sturgis rally held each year directly caused over 250 thousand covid-19 cases and cost $12 billion USD in healthcare costs. Not bad for a rally attended by an estimated 460 thousand people. The article even links to a similar PolitiFact article authored by Bill McCarthy on September 14, 2020. Judging by the dates the Poytner article seems to be directly referencing the PolitiFact article. It made it seem like this popular rally held in North Dakota had been a covid-19 hurricane that would cost billions of dollars in costs and countless lives.

Thankfully the PolitiFact article goes further and provides what flaws in the study by some critics. One such critic, cited in the article was Andrew Noymer. Per the article PolitiFact article, Noymer is an associate professor of population health and disease prevention at UC Irvine who provides this insight:

> *"Would there be 20% fewer cases of COVID in the United States? I think the answer is no. And the reason is because you're assuming that these people wouldn't have gotten it otherwise in a nation in which COVID is burning everywhere."* - Andrew Noymer, September 14, 2020 via PolitiFact

And Noymer wasn't the only critic of the study. Even Slate writer Jennifer Beam Dowd wasn't impressed by the report on the Sturgis rally. In an article published on September 10, 2020 titled, *The Sturgis Biker Rally Did Not Cause 266,796 Cases of covid-19*, Jennifer communicates we should all take a cautious approach to these claims by stating:

> *"There are lots of reasons to be skeptical of these findings, and the 266,796 number itself should raise serious believability alarm bells"*

Jennifer provides an excellent breakdown of how the initial report by Dhaval Dave and his colleagues was critically flawed. For example, Jennifer points out that Dhaval's report hadn't included a model for infectious disease transmission, which really should have been at the heart of any research regarding the transmission of an infectious disease. Jennifer continues by explaining more technical details about what Dhaval's study was missing and why it lacks the necessary rigor to be cited as a reliable source. It's an extremely well written article and reflective of a true journalist at work. The entire article provided me with some hope that there are real journalists doing investigative research to provide critical analysis of current affairs.

Dhaval's report was brought into the open, and subjected to skeptical review, and Li-meng Yan's report on the origin of covid-19 should be similarly reviewed. Neither their work, nor their voice should be silenced, and their unreviewed research certainly shouldn't be paraded around as a divisive fact by tribal political factions.

Date: June 26, 2020
Publisher: Vox
Writer: German Lopez
Headline: *The effect of Black Lives Matter protests on coronavirus cases, explained*

> *"Coronavirus cases are increasing, but Black Lives Matter protests may not be to blame. Here's why."* - German Lopez, June 26, 2020 via Vox.

The cognitive dissonance is glaring. For months, the public was told that large gatherings spread covid-19. Don't go to concerts, don't go to church, don't go to outdoor funerals. As recently as September 10, 2010 my family was told that my uncle, a U.S. Marine and Vietnam veteran with two combat deployments as a tunnel rat was not allowed to have a funeral, outdoors, with more than 10 people. A female employee at the Bakersfield National Cemetery was complicit in denying my uncle a funeral with all his remaining loved ones in attendance. She was just 'doing her job'. History is rarely kind to people who hide behind their job to justify immoral behaviour. I was furious, but my family complied, and I volunteered to give my spot up to some of my uncle's friends that knew him best.

Yet when the science doesn't fit the narrative as is the case with the black lives matter protests, it is easily discarded. Lopez identifies that public health experts warned that there was a risk the protests and riots from late May and early June would lead to a spike in covid-19. Lopez even acknowledges that a month later covid-19 cases were climbing, putting the U.S. in what would be the biggest spike of the pandemic. On July 24, the U.S. saw the largest single day surge of new cases at over 78 thousand. Part of this was due to increased testing, still there is a clear spike in numbers that correlates directly with the timing of the protests and riots led by BLM and antifa.

Lopez is quick to shift blame to everyone but the responsible parties. They use the ever-popular term, 'experts' and claim that states who had reopened indoor dining and bars were to blame for the spike in covid-19 cases. Lopez even has the audacity to make this statement:

> *"Studies show that previous measures to close down such gatherings likely helped lower Covid-19 cases."*

Gatherings like wide scale protests and rioting? I guess covid-19 hates all the smoke from the building fires the arsonists started. Data from Pennsylvania directly refutes this claim as the state experienced a similar spike, and yet ~~democratic Governor~~ Dear Leader Tom Wolf had kept the state under draconian lockdown through August. The irony is not lost on me that Dear Leader also took the opportunity to gladly violate his own unconstitutional orders for a photo op with BLM protestors. Must have been nice for Dear Leader to get in a photoshoot while Pennsylvania citizens suffered and thousands of families lost their homes, their livelihoods, and their lives. Lopez also continues in their argument by pointing out many of the protestors were young. Lopez's reasoning for pointing this out:

> *"It's not necessarily that young people transmit the coronavirus at lower rates. (The science is still out on that.) It's also not that young people aren't susceptible to the virus; there are examples of young people getting seriously sick and dying of Covid-19, with minority communities and people with preexisting conditions hit especially hard by the virus.*
>
> *But the research shows that young people, especially those without preexisting conditions, are much less likely to suffer the worst complications and die from the coronavirus."*

Again, for the first 3 months of the pandemic we were told masks protected not just us, but other people. So, I guess all those protesters were fine to risk their own lives, then spread the disease to everyone else, just like the Sturgis rally? Or was it only the Sturgis rally attendees that can spread covid-19? Doublespeak is confusing at times, so we'll cover that again. The liberal argument here is attempting to persuade people to believe that an estimated 15-25 million protestors had no discernable impact on the spread of an infectious disease. Yet just 2 months later the world is expected to believe that 450 thousand people at a biker rally caused a 20% increase in the total U.S. cases of covid-19 and cost the healthcare system billions of dollars. For anyone believes that tell the Easter Bunny I say hello.

Date: January 18, 2019
Publisher: CNN, Washington Post, NBCUniversal
Writer: various
Headline: various

Covington Catholic High School is a private Catholic school for boys in Park Hills, Kentucky. In January of 2019 they planned a field trip to Washington D.C. so students could attend a rally for the March for Life. Also, in D.C. that day was a group called the Black Hebrew Israelites. For those unfamiliar, the Anti-Defamation League identifies some sects of this group as anti-Semitic people who:

> *"...assert that white people are agents of Satan,*
> *Jews are liars and false worshipers of God,*
> *and blacks are the true chosen people and are*
> *racially superior to other ethnicities."*

They were at the Lincoln Memorial that day where they spent the morning taunting people, shouting insults at it seems to anyone who happened to walk by. When the Covington students began to gather near the Lincoln Memorial, after the March For Life rally, they too were greeted by the Black Hebrew Israelites. The group of Black Hebrew Israelites spared no venom that morning. They shouted racist slurs at the Covington students calling them incest babies, school shooters, crackers, and saying many other terrible things. Rather than react and escalate the situation, most of the students showed maturity and restraint. The students weren't their only victims that day. The Black Hebrew Israelites also targeted a group of Native Americans for insults, who were also in D.C. that day attending the Indigenous Peoples March.

As the three groups collided, tensions rose with the Covington students singing school songs to drown out the hateful messages being spewed at them. Sensing the increase in tension, Nathan Phillips wanted to intervene. And this is where things get dicey and confusing. Phillips then accused the Covington students for engaging in hateful and racist behaviour. In an interview with the Detroit Free Press he stated:

"These young men were beastly and these old black individuals was their prey, and I stood in between them and so they needed their pounds of flesh and they were looking at me for that."

In the same interview, Philips also accused the Covington students of attacking the Black Hebrew Israelites. Yet all the unedited video evidence tells a different story. Unfortunately, that real story didn't fit the preconstructed narrative. That day, many of the Covington students had committed a mortal sin in the eyes of the orange man bad gang. Some of the Covington students were wearing clothing in a show of support for President Trump.

With no consideration for journalistic curiosity or integrity, liberal media outlets ran the story Philips had constructed. That these white, MAGA hat wearing high school students had attacked not only a group of innocent black men, but also a group of Native Americans in D.C. that day to support the Indigineous Peoples March. CNN, Washington Post, NBCUniversal (as a parent company) all ran stories with inflammatory statements about these young students, with Nick Sandmann portrayed as the devil himself.

"Teens in Make America Great Again hats taunted a Native American elder at the Lincoln Memorial" - CNN, January 19, 2020

"Boys in 'Make America Great Again' Hats Mob Native Elder at Indigenous Peoples March" - the New York Times, January 19, 2020

Those were just some of the headlines run by the orange man bad machine. Afterall, Nick Sandmann had a red MAGA hat on, and stood silently, and patiently as he was attacked with insults by the Black Hebrew Israelites and was faced down by Nathan Philips. The students were condemned by democrat Alison Lundergan Grimes who was the Kentucky Secretary of State at the time. In commenting on the matter, she stated:

> *"I refuse to shame these children. Instead I turn to the adults that are teaching them and those that are silently letting others promote this behavior. This is not the Kentucky I know and love. We can do better and it starts with better leadership."*

People began sending bomb threats to the high school and making death threats against children. People were posting to their social media accounts saying they hoped the students and their families died. A university professor tweeted about Nick Sandmann:

> *"Honest question. Have you ever seen a more punchable face than this kid's?"* - @resaazlan, January 19, 2019

On January 20, a 90-minute video was released that showed and told a different story. Media outlets knew they had been baited by social media into running a false story. Switching gears and fearing the fall out CNN and the New York Times updated their headlines. Many media outlets ran retractions or updated their stories to reflect the full picture. But the damage had been done and many people still seethed with hate, attempting to put blame on Sandmann, his family, and Covington High School. Nick Sandmann and his family would not be intimidated or defamed. In February, his parents retained lawyers who began the slow process of filing lawsuits against the most egregious offenders. Washington Post, CNN, and NBCUniversal have all been named in separate filings. As of September 2020, both the Washington Post and CNN have settled out of court for an undisclosed amount.

chapter 12: platforms or publishers

In chapter 4 I questioned whether or not Twitter was just a platform, and I've attempted to limit my use of that term throughout the book. While companies like Facebook, Twitter, and reddit actively fight to keep that designation, in reality they look more and more like editing publishers each passing day. So why the distinction? What makes publishers different from platforms? Under the tenets of common-law a person or in this case a company who publishes a defamatory statement that was made by another bears the same liability for the statement. Meaning for example a book publisher or a newspaper publisher can be held liable for anything that appears within its published pages. The logic behind publisher liability is this: a publisher has some combination of knowledge, opportunity, or ability to exercise editorial discretion over the content of its publications.

Comparatively distributor liability is far more limited. Traditional media distributors such as libraries, bookstores, and newsstands are typically not liable for the content of the material that they simply distribute. The logic here is that they function more as resellers, and it would be impossible for distributors to read every publication before they sell or distribute it. It would shift responsibility for things like copyright and accuracy to the content distributors who are simply acting as a passthrough for the content creators. This would be a near impossible task as a distributor would lack the physical capability, technical expertise, subject matter knowledge, or details of a case to assert whether or not distributed content was true or false, or work copied from another source. For example, suppose I operated a newsstand and I sold the New York Times, Playboy, and Clinical Advisor, which is a monthly magazine written for nurses and physicians assistants. If I held liability as a distributor, I would need to fact check all the stories in the New York Times every day. Then I would need to make sure all the images in Playboy were properly licensed, legally obtained, and used with permission.

Finally, I would need to ensure all the information in Clinical Advisor was accurate, and matched prevailing medical practices in use by licensed medical professionals. As would every other newsstand owner. If forced to carry that burden distributors would be incentivized to engage in excessive self-censorship to protect against anything a content creator might have stated. Structurally it makes more sense to keep that liability with the publishers and content creators.

So, what legal responsibilities does a publisher have? That's a broad topic as publishing law is not a specific set of laws, rather it touches on several legal areas. Primarily when comparing to distributors the discussion would revolve around torts, intellectual property, and the First Amendment. Publishing is defined as:

> *"1) anything made public by print (as in a newspaper, magazine, pamphlet, letter, telegram, computer modem or program, poster, brochure or pamphlet), orally, or by broadcast (radio, television). 2) placing a legal notice in an approved newspaper of general publication in the county or district in which the law requires such notice to be published. 3) in the law of defamation (libel and slander) publication of an untruth about another only requires giving the information to a single person. Thus one letter can be the basis of a suit for libel, and telling one person is sufficient to show publication of slander." - West's Encyclopedia of American Law, edition 2, 2008 via The Gale Group*

Therefore, publishers are the people or companies that dispense information to the public. The content creator may or may not be the publisher. Legally, publishers can be held liable for mistakes, omissions, or falsehoods made by the content creator, as well as any mistakes, omissions, or falsehoods they might make as the publisher. Copyright and trademark issues are common things publishers must be wary of when publishing content. Defamation is also an area of concern. Publishers are responsible to ensure content they publish does not defame anyone. Any assertion of fact must be demonstrable, or the publisher may be subject to liabilities for publishing falsehoods.

Publishers are also responsible for not invading a person's reasonable expectations of privacy. Some content that violates this right can be subject to legal action if a person whose privacy sues to recover damages for the loss of privacy. This includes damages associated with mental and emotional distress suffered as a result of the loss of privacy, and specific injury or financial losses. It should be noted that public figures usually receive less privacy protections than private individuals.

Conversely, publishers also must ensure published content does not infringe a person's right of publicity. This includes a person's right to control the use of their likeness, name, and public persona. Usually this means the individual must have already been in the practice of using their likeness, name, or public person for commercial purposes. For example, a publisher may not use a celebrity's name, or likeness for advertising without prior consent.

When publishers run afoul of these legal boundaries there are often severe consequences. In chapter 11 one of the fake news stories described the circumstances surrounding Nick Sandmann. The publishers in this case were hit with numerous defamation lawsuits. Both CNN and the Washington Post opted to settle out of court. While the amount Nick and his family received was undisclosed, it's rumored to be in the tens of millions of dollars.

In March 2012 ABC published a report on a substance they referred to as 'pink slime' and its use in the commercial beef industry. ABC claimed that as much as 70% of commercial ground beef contained this substance. This report led to a defamation lawsuit filed against ABC by the company Beef Products, Inc. Initially filed in September of 2012 by 2017 Beef Products Inc was seeking $1.9 billion USD in damages. ABC finally agreed to settle, and while the amount is undisclosed the quarterly earnings report shows Walt Disney (ABC's parent company) paid over $177 million dollars towards litigation settlement. It's speculated that the settlement was for much more.

Know this makes digital tech firms extremely vested in retaining the title of platform. Because that designation provides special protections to these companies. It comes in the form of a section of the Communications Act of 1934. Formally codified as Section 230 of the Communications Act of 1934, section 230 is used to shield internet services from liabilities normally associated with being a publisher. Meaning Twitter would be considered more of a town square where any idiot can say terrible things, but ownership of the town square doesn't make Twitter in any way responsible for the idiot. It makes sense. On a platform each person should be responsible for their own actions and words. Specifically, section 230 states:

> *"No provider or user of an interactive computer service shall be treated as the publisher or speaker of any information provided by another information content provider."*

But that's not all it says. Section 230 continues with:

> *"No provider or user of an interactive computer service shall be held liable on account of any action voluntarily taken in good faith to restrict access to or availability of material that the provider or user considers to be obscene, lewd, lascivious, filthy, excessively violent, harassing, or otherwise objectionable, whether or not such material is constitutionally protected;"*

Republican Senator Ted Cruz believes that these digital tech companies have overstepped the bounds established by section 230. In an opinion article published by FoxNews on April 11, 2020 Senator Cruz states:

> *"in order to be protected by Section 230, companies like Facebook should be 'neutral*

*public forums'. On the flip side, they should be
considered to be a 'publisher or speaker' of
user content if they pick and choose what gets
published or spoken."*

Senator Cruz continues in his reasoning with these
thoughts:

> *As I expressed to Mark Zuckerberg, as a
> private business Facebook has a clear First
> Amendment right to publish whatever it wants
> on its website within the bounds of the law.
> The company can support political causes and
> oppose ones it disagrees with, just like a
> private citizen can speak his or her mind or
> agitate against opposing views.*
>
> *But if Facebook is busy censoring legal,
> protected speech for political reasons, the
> company should be held accountable for the
> posts it lets through. And it should not enjoy
> any special congressional immunity from
> liability for its actions.*

It isn't just Senator Cruz who believes this. While it's hard
to believe there was a time before the internet existed. In
that time, courts and common law held that newsstands,
bookstores, and libraries, the analog equivalents of reddit,
Facebook, and Twitter today, were not responsible for, and
had no duty to ensure that every book, magazine, and
newspaper they distributed was not defamatory or
otherwise published without consent. When the internet
became popular, and the technology was still new to the
general public, judges applied this same logic to online
platforms, and extended similar protections.

In a 1991 lawsuit Cubby v. CompuServe, the court
ruled that because internet companies didn't have editorial
involvement, these companies should be treated as
distributors, rather than publishers when determining
liability during a defamation lawsuit. Federal law recognizes

that a publisher who repeats or republishes defamatory content has the same liability as the original publisher of the content. Treating internet companies as distributors provided statutory protection.

Just three years later in 1994 that outlook would change when Prodigy's Money Talk bulletin board became central to a claim by Stratton Oakmont. In their suit, Stratton Oakmont president Danny Porush alleges an unidentified user at the bulletin board posted several comments suggesting Danny Porush had committed fraud in connection with the initial public offering of stock of Solomon-Page, Ltd. Stratton Oakmont sued Prodigy Services Co. and the unidentified user for defamation. In their ruling, a federal judge found that Prodigy was liable for content posted on its message boards because Prodigy advertised that it removed obscene posts. The judge ruled in favor of Stratton Oakmont, stating that Prodigy's curation of content made Prodigy more like a publisher than a library. The irony is not lost that Danny Porush later pled guilty to securities fraud and money laundering. Stratton Oakmont may sound familiar because it was the company central to the movie The Wolf of Wall Street.

Of course, this ruling conflicted with the earlier federal court ruling in Cubby v. CompuServe. However, there was one key difference between the two cases. The judge noted that because Prodigy engaged in content screening it therefore exercised editorial control. If not for section 230 being signed into law in 1996, these two cases had the potential to create a supreme court showdown to decide the fate of the internet.

But section 230 doesn't give internet companies carte blanche. In a court ruling issued in 2015 for the case Song Fi Inc. v. Google Inc, Judge Samuel Conti stated that:

> *"As a threshold matter, YouTube argues it is entitled to statutory immunity from Plaintiffs' breach of contract and tortious interference claims because "Luv ya" and its allegedly artificially inflated view count are "otherwise objectionable" within the meaning of Section*

230(c)(2) of the Communications Decency Act. See 47 U.S.C. § 230(c)(2). However, because the Court finds neither the plain meaning of "otherwise objectionable" nor the context, purpose, or history of the Communications Decency Act support YouTube's interpretation of "otherwise objectionable," YouTube is not entitled to statutory immunity from Plaintiffs' breach of contract or tortious interference claims."

Judge Conti continues in their ruling by stating:

"...Congress did not intended "otherwise objectionable" to refer to (as YouTube believes) anything which it finds undesirable for any reason."

This wasn't the only case that called into question whether an internet company had broad discretion to censor content at will. In 2009 the 9th circuit court of appeals issued a 2-1 ruling in the case Zango, Inc. v. Kaspersky Lab Inc. The court's ruling opinion written by Judge Pamela Ann Rymer stated that Kaspersky Inc was protected from liability by section 230. However, in writing their concurring opinion, Judge Raymond Fisher stated that:

"But under the generous coverage of § 230(c)(2)(B)'s immunity language, a blocking software provider might abuse that immunity to block content for anticompetitive purposes or merely at its malicious whim, under the cover of considering such material "otherwise objectionable." Focusing for the moment on anticompetitive blocking, I am concerned that blocking software providers who flout users' choices by blocking competitors' content could hide behind § 230(c)(2)(B) when the competitor seeks to recover damages. I doubt Congress intended § 230(c)(2)(B) to be so forgiving."

There has been a growing movement to strip section 230 protections stripped from companies who act as publishers with their biased editorial style. It seems Judge Fisher was correct about Congress's intentions. Just 9 years later members of congress would begin to take notice and begin to take action. Vocal in his disappointment with large tech firms U.S. Senator Josh Hawley had this to say:

> *"With Section 230, tech companies get a sweetheart deal that no other industry enjoys—complete exemption from traditional publisher liability in exchange for providing a forum free of political censorship. Unfortunately, and unsurprisingly, big tech has failed to hold up its end of the bargain."*

In an effort to curb section 230 abuses correctly identified by Judge Fisher and Judge Conti Senator Hawley took action and in June 2019 he introduced the Ending Support for Internet Censorship Act. This legislation is designed to remove immunity for companies like Twitter, Facebook, and Google, who have weaponized section 230 as a way to silence political dissent. In the bill it states that companies that wish to retain their immunity must demonstrate they do not act to moderate content in a politically biased way. Specifically, the bill states:

> *the provider does not (and, during the 2-year period preceding the date on which the provider submits the application for certification, did not) moderate information provided by other information content providers in a politically biased manner.*

The bill then defines what politically biased moderation:

> *"The moderation practices of a provider of an interactive computer service are politically*

*biased if the provider moderates information
provided by other information content providers
in a manner that is designed to negatively
affect a political party, political candidate, or
political viewpoint; or disproportionately
restricts or promotes access to, or the
availability of, information from a political
party, political candidate, or political viewpoint;
or an officer or employee of the provider makes
a decision about moderating information
provided by other information content providers
that is motivated by an intent to negatively
affect a political party, political candidate, or
political viewpoint."*

Senator Hawley's legislative approach may be the only recourse against companies who continually overstep their bounds. The Office of the Attorney General submitted a bill on September 23, 2020 that proposed legislation to amend section 230. The bill was based on the same recommendations they made in a report released in June 2020. Based on this report, the proposed legislation creates carve outs for: bad actor companies intentionally hosting illegal content, child exploitation, cyberstalking, and terrorism. The bill would also remove immunity for companies that have or receive direct notice; or had prior knowledge that content posted by a third party was illegal. One interesting section specifically mentions Stratton Oakmont in reference to the court case mentioned earlier. The bill proposes that:

*"DOJ proposes to revise (c)(1) to include a new
subparagraph (C) which would clarify that any
content-moderation decision made by a
provider in good faith and consistent with its
terms of service does not, on its own, render a
platform a speaker or publisher for all other
third-party content on its service. This
subsection would make clear that Stratton
Oakmont v. Prodigy Services Co., 1995 WL*

> *323710 (N.Y. Sup. Ct. 1995) continues to be
> explicitly overruled and avoids the "Moderator's
> Dilemma" in which a platform faces increased
> liability for good faith moderation of offensive
> content."*

This section makes it clear that nobody is seeking to force Facebook, reddit, or Twitter to become fully liable publishers. Rather Senator Cruz, Senator Hawley, President Trump, Attorney General Barr, and millions of other conservative voices are saying loudly: be a distributor not a publisher.

Conservative leaders are not the only politicians taking notice. Increasingly social media companies are faced with criticisms regarding terrorist content and hate speech. This is highlighted by the terrorist attack in Christchurch, New Zealand, which was live streamed on Facebook. Political figures from the left including Nancy Pelosi and Elizabeth Warren have questioned the apparent lack of action to curb this type of content.

The fact that Twitter, Facebook, Google, and similar digital tech companies got their start as internet companies should not preclude them from being considered publishers. CNN, MSNBC, and FoxNews all have an internet presence with the various websites they own. Yet the content published on their websites seem to be treated differently than content published by Twitter, Facebook, and Google. Why this differentiation?

One observation is that traditional media outlets such as CNN and Fox pay for content to then be published on their website. They are assuming the responsibility of being a publisher when they are actively engaged in curating content. Isn't that Senator Cruz, and Senator Hawley's point? When Facebook engaged and contracted a company to curate via fact check content posted on their platform, they moved away from simply being a pass-through distributor for content providers. Facebook asserts truth value to the content posted to their pages much as a newspaper or book publisher would fact check the content within their respective pages. Remember the newsstand example earlier in the chapter? That's exactly what Facebook is attempting to do. When Facebook exercises their version of editorial discretion, they actively seek to moderate the content of its pages to craft a specific on brand message. This is fundamentally separate from distributing and moderating to remove illegal, obscene, lewd, lascivious, filthy, excessively violent, harassing, or otherwise objectionable content. By taking refuge in section 230 they seek a competitive advantage over similar publishers which has created market conditions to unduly favor a company simply because it only publishes on the internet.

YouTube acts similarly by removing content they deem misinformation. For example, when they took down content posted to their website with covid-19 information that dissented from their preferred narratives they were functionally performing the duties of a publisher. Here YouTube took a second stance in claiming opinions provided by medical experts from one group were more valid than another. This is not the act of a distributor. This more closely aligns with actions a publisher would take.

Further Facebook, reddit, YouTube, Google, all act as publishers when they take editorial actions in bias censoring and fact checking against conservative voices. It's these intentional actions that go beyond the scope of a distribution platform that lawmakers and the public find so disturbing. It's the equivalent of a library prominently featuring economics books written by Karl Marx and claiming Thomas Sowell's books are misleading and then banning them. Section 230 was intended to provide respite for platforms who remove, in good faith, content that is illegal or otherwise obscene, lewd, lascivious, filthy, excessively violent, harassing, or otherwise objectionable. The goal here was to prevent platforms from having to curate countless amounts of content posted by its users creating the moderator's dilemma.

Hopefully, society can find a way to remove protections from companies who abuse this institutional immunity and still provide enough latitude to innovate. Some lawmakers believe additional legislation to close the section 230 loophole will force these companies to become fairer and more balanced when moderating content. I lack their optimism. The law of unintended consequences supersedes all others, and despite anyone's best intentions I feel like digital tech companies will do their best to push the boundaries of whatever comes next. Afterall, corporate media outlets have figured out a way to survive for decades. To be honest I'm not entirely certain what a real solution looks like other than imploring these digital platforms to stop their biased censorship and engage in more ethical practices. Their current disinformation strategy appears to be accelerating society ever closer to a precipice of disaster.

chapter 13: ramblings of an American

This is more of a postscript than a chapter, but hey it's my book. Anyone that made it this far gets to read some more ramblings of a fed up American. The liberal democrat attempts to control information are not shocking, but it is the greatest threat to humanity since the rise of communism. The insidious nature of this type of tyranny is what I find most disturbing. It's thought control, straight out of an Orwellian nightmare. To avoid the dystopian future I fear is hurtling towards us, it is incumbent upon each person to keep themselves informed, do their best to inform others, learn to be independent and rational thinkers, and teach their children to be independent and rational thinkers as well. It's a monumental task and a huge burden of responsibility. The only real question each person must ask themselves is: is the effort worth it?

While I can't answer the question for anyone but myself, to be honest, writing this didn't take much investigative research. I used DuckDuckGo to find most of the articles I cited. Which is kind of the point I'm trying to make regarding the lack of journalistic integrity displayed by the entire industry, and why their bias is so easy to demonstrate: they're fucking lazy. These articles, this deceptive journalism it's generally not even well written or well-reasoned. It's easy to identify and tear down by anyone who takes the time to read beyond these divisive headlines. This book is an attempt at helping people realize how prevalent this political bias is by exposing the resurgence of yellow journalism perpetrated by the orange man bad gang. I wanted this book to shed some light on the subject so that they may reevaluate their previous assumptions and develop a more informed opinion. By that I don't mean they must necessarily change their politics, though for personal reasons that would be nice, but I do hope at the very least it forces those who vehemently disagree with me politically to form more consistent, and rational arguments. I promise you if you come at me with some CNN or FoxNews bullshit talking point while I'm sitting in the bar, it will not end well for you. Or maybe it will, to be honest I only keep up with an extremely narrow band of subjects I'm interested in.

I think I've established through a preponderance of evidence, circumstantial and otherwise, that yes, corporate media, and the majority of big tech firms do have a liberal bias and liberal agenda. What does that mean to you? Do you trust these corporations to tell you how to think? If you're okay with that idea, great. I am not okay with any of it because I do not trust them, and my answer would be the same even if these companies had a conservative bias. It's less that I wouldn't align with their decision making in such a scenario, it's that I worry what would happen when the shoe is on the other foot. For my critics out there, who correctly point out my bias is present throughout my book, of course it is. I clearly find marxists, communists, and socialists ideals repugnant. I'm pointing out a systemic problem in news media reporting and censorship perpetrated by the orange man bad gang through that lens. Feel free to tell me how I cherry picked all the articles, headlines, and quotes. You're right. I did. There's probably an avalanche of quotes, articles, and headlines where conservatives have perpetrated the same crimes. You know, on all the conservative leaning big tech companies like.... go ahead and name a few. I'll wait.

The difference between having a political bias, and using that bias to silence others, is I am willing to listen to counter arguments. I'll sit down and discuss why I have a different analysis of the facts presented. I welcome differing viewpoints. What I will not do is lie, misrepresent, or outright silence the people who have them. Silencing dissent is a serious threat to a free society. When Facebook, Twitter, reddit, Google, and all the other companies that engage in this behaviour, they should be condemned.

For all the vitriol spewed about President Trump, he was the inevitable outcome following 8 years of Obama's divisive rhetoric and politics. The shoe is on the other foot, and all the things libertarians warned democrats not to cheer Obama for doing appear to be fulfilling nightmares for democrats under President Trump. In November of 2013 Senator Mitch McConnell issued a dire warning to

Democrats, *"I say to my friends on the other side of the aisle, you'll regret this, and you may regret it a lot sooner than you think."* This warning was issued because the Majority Leader at the time, Harry Reid, voted to change the rules of the Senate that allowed presidential nominees for Cabinet members and federal judges could advance with a simple majority. Three years later Mitch McConnel was proved correct when President Trump was elected, and since he took office, he has appointed over 190 judges with lifelong tenures to federal courts. This outpaces all other presidents, and if this trend continues through 2024, he's on track to break 400. The shoe is on the other foot.

For the record, I have never voted for a Republican prior to 2020. I have voted a few times. After coming out of the Bush presidency deeply disappointed, I voted for Obama out of frustration. I should have realized that a democrat would not sit by and allow themselves to be upstaged by a republican. Obama somehow delivered four years worse than Bush's entire eight. Then out of disappointment I voted for nobody in 2012. In 2016 I re-registered to vote in Philadelphia as a Libertarian and voted for Gary Johnson. I re-registered in Philadelphia because it was my new home, and I was previously registered to vote in my hometown of Bakersfield, California. While I was in the military I moved around and utilized absentee voting for the 2008 election. I remain a registered Libertarian, though I am less and less excited by that party as many of the members exhibit the disturbing trait of needing ideological purity (much like the current Democratic Party). I'm reminded of the expression, don't throw the baby out with the bath water.

Some people reading this book will rabidly disagree with me and everything I've written, but I don't think that's a bad thing. I embrace civil discourse. Show me where I'm wrong, explain to me where I took missteps in my observations. Often, I find it's the refuge of a failed argument to simply say, "do your research" or to cite some alleged expert. I'm not asking about some expert's opinion. To be honest I've probably read their analysis of the situation and concluded they were wrong. What reasonable explanation can you show me that is different? How can you convince me I'm wrong? Can you form your own perspective and ask me to view things through that lens as well? If the answer is no, then you're not thinking for yourself, you're parroting back talking points from your parents, your professors, or worse, whatever corporate news media channel your political ideologies subscribe to. Think for yourself. Do your own analysis of the facts and circumstances for the topic at hand and tell me why you think I'm wrong. We'll get some beers, and I'll listen.

I would also like to offer some advice. Conservatives need to do a better job at supporting one another. Several times I mention ideological purity tests as a severe moral failing of the liberal agenda. The notion that if a party member isn't woke enough, the woke mob gestapo will tear them down. One of the wedges the progressive movement drives between their supporters is the never-ending push for ideological purity. Newsflash: nobody is that good, and nobody will ever be that good. Its why liberals tear each other down more than anyone else. They eat their own. All of us are human and we're going to make mistakes, we're going to say things out of frustration or anger, and we're going to make decisions that don't have the expected outcome. That means when a comedian like Sarah Silverman did a skit wearing black face over a decade ago, it probably wasn't done with hate in her heart. As much as I dislike Sarah's brand of comedy, I sincerely doubt she's secretly attending klan rallies and wants the south to rise again. I advise conservatives not to follow the same path and evaluate for themselves if a B+ political candidate is good enough, or at least better than a D-. No politician will ever be exactly who you want them to be. They should generally be pointed in the right direction with no expectation that they'll never take a misstep, or you will never disagree with them.

Also, for conservatives, I would like to see more ventures into creating alternative channels for the flow of information. Apps like Parler, Righter, and spaces like theDonald.win. Utilize the free market to win back freedom of speech, and freedom of thought. Think of it like the

1980's made in America call to action, only for the digital age. Don't just use these spaces to shitpost, and troll. Conservatives should really develop a market space that addresses all our collective complaints about Twitter, Google, and Facebook. In the span of 20 years, Google redefined how people understood the internet, Amazon reshaped the face of retail, Apple reshaped the very idea of a phone (and in the process the very face of society), Twitter changed how we communicate, and Facebook changed how we stay connected (with all the people we went to high school with apparently). Do not be so short sighted to believe these companies can't be challenged, or displaced. Advocate for, and support companies that defend the free exchange of ideas, not just through words, but through actions. In the spaces that exist, support conservative thinkers, conservative content, and conservative voices. These are the ways you can push back and reclaim not just your individual freedoms but how you push back against communist agitators like antifa. It's how you retake America and help people know it's the greatest nation on earth. Head's up, I get a little rough in the next paragraph.

I also have some advice for the more liberal readers. Yall need to slow the fuck down. Not one of you is ready for all that defund the police, tear it all down, blow it all up, riot in the street, civil war, crazy ass shit you been talking. That big dick energy you think you got, it ain't there fam so you need to calm your little asses down. That means when your liberal buddies start saying some shit like:

> *"If they even TRY to replace RBG we burn the entire fucking thing down."* - @rezaaslan, September 18, 2020

> *"Burn Congress down before letting Trump try to appoint anyone to SCOTUS"* - @EmmMacfarlane, September 18, 2020

> *"If McConnell jams someone through, which he will, there will be riots."* - @LEBassett, September 18, 2020

"Fucking A, Ed. If you can't shut it down, burn it down." - @rossacrosswi, September 18, 2020

"Fuck no. Burn it all down." - @DaddyFiles, September 18, 2020

"Ruth Bader Ginsburg's body isn't even cold and Mitch McConnell is dancing on her grave. This is war. Dems have powerful weapons. Now is the time to use them." - @robreiner, September 19, 2020

"Mount up. You dare try and replace her right now and there will be war. That's a promise. Signed, Us #RBG" - @RussTamblyn, September 18, 2020

You need to grab them up, look them dead in the eyes, and tell them to shut fuck up, and sit their little protein deficient asses down. No the fuck you don't want a civil war. First of all, we've all seen the mugshots of the antifa and BLM rioters that have been arrested. I thought they were headshots for Gollum auditions. Apparently yall only come in two sizes, childhood famine survivor, and Grimace from McDonald's. Yall look like the all-star lineup from the isle of misfit eating disorders. I've seen more muscular jelly fish washed up on the beach. You are not physically or mentally prepared for the violence of war.

Yall was putting tourniquets on people for non-bleeding rubber bullet bruises. There are videos of liberals literally crying and claiming PTSD from firing an AR-15. As a reminder, that 17-year-old boy in Kenosha with an AR-15 planted three antifa rioters who violently attacked him. Then you called the police. You couldn't make it through two months of riots without calling the police. Think about all those things before you start puffing your chest spouting that, "I wear grown up pants now so we going to war" nonsense. Also think about the fact that conservatives have way more guns and most of them have been hunting. Most of the military is or leans conservative, and that means most veterans are not on your side. You already pissed off all the police departments with your defund the police nonsense, and ACAB bullshit. You've been allowed to roam free in cities like Seattle and Portland by feckless politicians. This has given you a false sense of security that nobody will fight back. I assure you there are some cold cranking, bad mother fuckers out there violently prepared to bash your skull in or shoot you in the face. And they have been doing two things for the past decade: training and waiting. They are praying you start some real shit so they can put all their training to use. Most of us are just going to sit by, and watch it all happen, and then call the cops and the paramedics we didn't ask to be defunded when it's over. I beg you, please do not give these people a reason strap in. This is would be a terrible, terrible idea for you. You don't want this smoke. I beg of you, use your words. If your ideas are so good, then it should be an easy argument to demonstrate with factual evidence, and real world results your ideas for governance are better. But if you're dead set on going down the path of violence and starting your war, **fuck around and find out.**

Finally, I would like to offer this advice to liberal and left leaning individuals who would like to see more general support for their policy agenda. I would advise against the practices described throughout this book. It has been a failing strategy. Telling people what and how to think has been a failing strategy. Censoring dissenting, and conservative viewpoints has been a failing strategy. Intentionally deceptive editing news footage has been a failing strategy. Especially when raw video footage is so prevalent in today's media, the willful use of manipulated video clips hurts your cause more than you might think. President Trump is stronger than ever. The four-year experiment of identity politics failed to produce your desired result.

I highly, highly recommend a different approach. Try engaging with the people you disagree with. Try talking to them. Counter their arguments with rational, thoughtful, genuine discussion. Apply some logical consistency to your arguments. If insulting someone's race or ethnicity is racist, make sure that also applies to liberals who hate white people. If it's sexism to discriminate based on gender, make sure you call it out when it happens to men. If it's bigotry to discriminate based on sexual orientation, make sure your allies aren't tweeting that straight white men are the worst. Making enemies out of people you're asking to support you is probably not going to help achieve your goals. To quote Milton Friedman from his 1962 work, *Capitalism and Freedom*:

> *"…I believe strongly that the color of a man's skin or the religion of his parents is, by itself, no reason to treat him differently; that a man should be judged by what he is and what he does and not by these external characteristics. I deplore what seem to me the prejudice and narrowness of outlook of those whose tastes differ from mine in this respect and I think less of them for it. But in a society based on free discussion, the appropriate recourse is for me to seek to persuade them that their tastes are bad and that they should change their views and their behavior, not to use coercive power to enforce my tastes and my attitudes on others."*